CW00430243

Welcome...

"I love all forms of photography, but nothing comes close to the passion and enthusiasm that I have for portraiture. Whether it is photographing family or friends, shooting contemporary lifestyle images or capturing candids, I always enjoy the challenge of delivering high quality, creative and appealing portraits. I've been lucky in my job to work with many of the UK's leading portrait photographers, who have provided me with a wealth of expert advice, techniques and skills that have improved my own photography. Many of these leading pros were involved in the tutorials and guides in this *Essential Guide to Portraits*, so you too will also benefit from their mastery of portraiture. As you'll discover, taking great portraits doesn't demand you have the most expensive and extensive camera outfit, a budget DSLR with a 50mm lens is all you need to take brilliant images. What's more important is having a good eye for composition and detail, knowing the basic techniques to lighting, whether you're using be daylight or flash, and above all, developing strong interpersonal skills with your subject. Don't underestimate this latter point – a relaxed, happy subject will always make for better portraits, so ensure you are confident, friendly and have fun while you're taking pictures. All the best!"

DANIEL LEZANO, EDITOR

Meet our portrait experts

All our portrait experts are regular contributors to *Digital SLR Photography* magazine. For further advice and inspiration to help you improve your photo skills, pick up the latest issue, available on the second Tuesday of every month. For more information, visit: www.digitalslrphoto.com

DANIEL LEZANO
An enthusiast photographer for over 25 years, Daniel specialises in portraiture and is author of several books, including *100 Ways to Take Better Portrait Photographs*.

BRETT HARKNESS
Brett is one of the UK's leading portrait and social photographers and runs regular photo workshops. For further details, visit: www.brettharkness.com

BJORN THOMASSEN
Bjorn is a successful portrait photographer, a master of lighting and leading speaker at seminars and courses. For more information, visit: www.bjornatinspire.com

PAUL WARD
Paul is a professional portrait and fashion photographer who specialises in location and studio shoots. For more details, visit: www.paulwardphotography.com

The Essential Guide to Portraits

This second edition of *The Essential Guide to Portraits* has been published with a choice of four stunning covers. We'd be interested to know which is your favourite. Please let us know by visiting our website and making your choice on our online poll. We'll choose one name at random from the entries who will receive a free Cokin filter kit worth over £40!

Produced by *Digital SLR Photography* at:
6 Swan Court, Cygnet Park,
Peterborough, Cambs PE7 8GX
Phone: 01733 567401. Fax 01733 352650
Email: enquiries@digitalslrphoto.com
Online: www.digitalslrphoto.com

Editorial
To contact editorial phone: 01733 567401

Editor **Daniel Lezano**
daniel_lezano@dennis.co.uk

Art Editor **Luke Marsh**
luke_marsh@dennis.co.uk

Designer **Luke Medler**
luke_medler@dennis.co.uk

Editorial Co-ordinator **Jo Lezano**
jo_lezano@dennis.co.uk

Editorial contributors: Brett Harkness, Matty Graham, Ross Hoddinott, Paul Stefan, Bjorn Thomassen, Paul Ward & Caroline Wilkinson

Advertising & Production
Display & Classified Sales: 0207 907 6651
Advertising Sales **Guy Scott-Wilson**
guy_scott-wilson@dennis.co.uk
Sales Executive **Joshua Rouse**
joshua_rouse@dennis.co.uk
Production Controller **Dan Stark**
dan_stark@dennis.co.uk

Publishing & Marketing
NICKY BAKER DIGITAL PRODUCTION MANAGER
DHARMESH MISTRY BOOKAZINE MANAGER
ROBIN RYAN PRODUCTION DIRECTOR
JULIAN LLOYD-EVANS MD OF ADVERTISING
DAVID BARKER NEWSTRADE DIRECTOR
BRETT REYNOLDS CHIEF OPERATING OFFICER
IAN LEGGETT GROUP FINANCE DIRECTOR
JAMES TYE CHIEF EXECUTIVE
FELIX DENNIS CHAIRMAN

recycle When you've finished enjoying this magazine please recycle

CONTENTS

TURN TO PAGE 129 TO FIND OUT ABOUT OUR FANTASTIC SUBSCRIPTION OFFERS

Setting up your DSLR

Your digital SLR has a bewildering array of features and while this is great in some respects, the choice can lead to confusion about which settings to select to suit a particular shooting scenario. Here we explain the key tools of your DSLR you need to know when trying to shoot portraits

EXPOSURE MODE Don't think about using the Portrait program mode – you're more than a happy snapper if you're reading this guide. Instead, select aperture-priority AE mode (A or Av), which lets you choose the aperture, while automatically setting the appropriate shutter speed. For most types of portraiture, you'll want to use a wide aperture to throw the background out of focus. To start off, use f/5.6, as this blurs the background but gives enough depth-of-field to keep the entire face (eyes, nose and ears) in focus. By selecting aperture-priority, you'll be using ambient light only. While flash has its uses, using (and controlling) daylight will give you more natural results and help you learn to manipulate available light.

ISO RATING & THE RECIPROCAL RULE In terms of quality, the lower the ISO the better, so we would recommend you set ISO 100 or 200 to begin with. Hand-holding your DSLR will allow you more freedom to move around and shoot candids, but watch out for camera shake. The simplest way to do this is to use the reciprocal rule. All this means is you shouldn't let your shutter speed drop below the reciprocal of the lens you're using. Sounds complicated but it isn't. If you're using the lens at 100mm then ensure the shutter speed is above 1/100sec to reduce the risk of shake. If you're using the lens at 200mm then make sure the shutter speed is above 1/200sec, etc. Easy, eh!

Increasing the ISO rating is an easy way to achieve a faster shutter speed to avoid shake. Try to avoid going above ISO 800 as otherwise you'll notice increased noise in the image. In low light, whenever possible, we'd recommend you use a tripod. It allows you to use a lower ISO rating as shutter speeds aren't such a concern, while also helping with composition.

WHITE BALANCE You should set the White Balance to the lighting conditions you're shooting in. If you're working in mixed light and are a little unsure, then Auto (AWB) is the best compromise. Of course, if you're shooting Raw, you can always change the White Balance when you open the image on your computer. Something to bear in mind is that setting the wrong WB preset can be used to purposely shift the colour balance. For instance, setting Cloudy in daylight will add warmth to the tones, while selecting Tungsten will result in a very cool, blue cast. Be creative.

IMAGE QUALITY We would recommend you shoot Raw, as it will allow you to play with settings, particularly White Balance later. If your camera has a facility to shoot Raw + JPEG, use it with JPEG set to 'Small/Basic'. Then when you're reviewing images, you can go through the small JPEGs quickly, choose your favourites and work on the appropriate Raw files. If you're confident in your ability, and don't expect to need to make tweaks to the exposure or White Balance in post-production, opt for the best quality JPEG for optimum results and to save room on your memory card.

AUTOFOCUS With the vast majority of portraits, it's important that the eyes of your subject are sharply in focus because, more often than not, they're the main focal point. Your camera most likely has multi-point AF, which allows you to choose between leaving all the AF points active or to select individual AF points. You could leave all the AF points active to ensure you don't miss a great shot, but you run the risk that you'll not focus on the eyes and instead catch the nose as it's the nearest object to the camera.

A better option is to select a single AF point and use this to focus on the eye. The central AF sensor is usually the most sensitive, so you can use this to lock the AF by placing the central AF point over one of the subject's eyes, then pressing the shutter button halfway down. Once the AF is locked, recompose and fire. It sounds tricky, but with practice it will become second nature. Another option is to select the AF point that sits over the subject's eye in the frame. Doing this means that you don't have to recompose so much, allowing you to work quicker. This is a better option if you intend to rattle off a sequence of shots with a very similar composition. If you do intend to lock the focus, remember to ensure that your camera is set to single-shot AF as otherwise you won't be able to lock on your subject's eye.

METERING Your digital SLR's multi-zone meter should be capable of exposing portraits perfectly in most situations. Take a test shot, check the screen and use the exposure compensation facility to add/subtract a little exposure if you feel the shot is too dark or light. Where your camera's multi-zone meter may falter is if your subject has very light or dark skin tones, is wearing light or dark clothing or is strongly backlit. In these situations, either use exposure compensation, or select the spot meter and use the AE-L (Auto-Exposure Lock) button to take a reading from a mid-tone in the scene, or from an 18% grey card that you place near the subject.

Setting up your DSLR for portraits

A little unsure how to select the exposure, White Balance or AF systems on your digital SLR? Let us show you the way via five popular DSLRs

CANON EOS 450D/500D/550D

(1) Set the top-plate dial to Av to select aperture-priority.
(2) Press the ISO button to set a rating.
(3) Use the WB button to choose White Balance and the AF button to set AF to One-Shot AF.
(4) Press MENU and select the metering option on the second tab: we recommend Evaluative.
(5) To set image quality, press MENU and select Quality in the first tab.

EOS 550D and EOS 600D only: Press the Q button and use the four-way control buttons as a shortcut to all these key functions.

NIKON D3100/D5100

(1) Set the top-plate dial to A to select aperture-priority.

(2) Press the info (i) button and scroll to metering mode and select your choice with the four-way control. We'd suggest you start with Matrix. Press the info (i) button again and select AF Mode to AF-S.

(3) Set the ISO rating, White Balance and image quality using the same procedure.

OLYMPUS E-400/410/420

(1) Set the top-plate dial to A to select aperture-priority. The other settings are made using the Fn button, four-way controller and the OK button.

(2) To set the autofocus, press OK, select AF, and set S-AF.For metering, press OK, go to the metering icon, select multi-zone and press OK. Set the ISO rating, White Balance and image quality using the same procedure.

PENTAX K-SERIES

(1) Set the top-plate dial to Av to select aperture-priority.

(2) Press the Fn button and press right on the four-way control to select an ISO rating, followed by OK to set.

(3) Press left to set the White Balance in the same way.

(4) To choose the AF mode, press MENU and the Rec. Mode tab, go down to AF mode, then right to set (we recommend AF-S). Set the metering mode in the same way (we recommend multi-zone). Image quality is also set this way.

SONY ALPHA: MOST MODELS

(1) Set the exposure dial on the left of the top-plate to A for aperture-priority.

(2) Press MENU and on the first tab select the image quality (preferably Raw & JPEG). The following settings are selected using the Fn button and the four-way control on the rear.

(3) Press Fn, go to Metering mode and select Multi segment. Press Fn, go to AF mode and set AF-S. Press Fn, go to White Balance and choose a setting.

(3) Press the ISO button and set the ISO rating you wish to use.

OUR RECOMMENDED CAMERA SETTINGS FOR SHOOTING PORTRAITS
Exposure mode: Aperture-priority set to f/5.6 to begin with
Metering Pattern: Multi-zone
Autofocus: Use a single AF sensor with AF mode set to single-shot (AF-S)
White Balance: Match lighting conditions
Image Quality: Raw + JPEG
ISO rating: ISO 100 or 200

The basics of exposure

Our jargon-free guide to the fundamentals of exposure provides everything you need to know to get to grips with apertures and shutter speeds

If you're new to digital SLR photography, it's essential that you understand the fundamentals of exposure. Every exposure you take is made up of a combination of an aperture and shutter speed that determines how much light will reach the sensor. The aperture is the iris in the lens, much like the pupil of the eye, which can widen to allow more light through or contract to restrict the amount of light that enters the lens. Use a wide aperture and more light is able to pass through during a set time span than if you had selected a small aperture setting.

The shutter is a barrier in front of the sensor that moves out of the light's path when you press the shutter release, allowing light to reach the sensor and expose an image. The duration of the exposure is determined by the shutter speed. There is an obvious relationship between the aperture and the shutter speed in determining the correct exposure and this is selected by the exposure mode. While a Full Auto mode provides point-and-shoot simplicity by automatically selecting a combination of aperture and shutter speed, and allows beginners to take great pictures with the minimum of fuss, the beauty and enjoyment of digital SLR photography is to take control and directly determine how the picture will look.

The first major step to doing this is to take your camera off Full Auto and select one of the exposure modes that allow for far more creative photography. Follow our guide and experiment with apertures and shutter speeds – after all, it's not like you'll be wasting any film! Before you know it, you'll soon be creating imaginative images rather than just shooting snaps.

Exposure controls

Many beginners believe it's difficult to use aperture- or shutter-priority mode but in fact it's very easy to do. Once you've selected the exposure mode (1), it's simply a case of rotating the input dial (2) until the aperture or shutter speed you'd like to use appears on the top-plate (or rear) LCD panel (3). Depress the shutter button halfway and the camera works out the rest. It's as easy as that!

UNDERSTANDING SHUTTER SPEEDS

Exposure settings are made by changing either the aperture or the shutter speed. The increments at which you change these settings are normally referred to as 'stops'. When you change a setting by a 'stop', you are either doubling or halving the exposure. So for instance, changing from 1/500sec to 1/250sec doubles the duration of the exposure. As well as full stops, you can also vary exposure in 1/2 or 1/3 stops depending on the camera model you use. The diagram below shows shutter speeds from one second to 1/4000sec.

Full stops	1sec	1/2sec	1/4sec	1/8sec	1/16sec	1/30sec	1/60sec	1/125sec	1/250sec	1/500sec	1/1000sec	1/2000sec	1/4000sec
Half stops	0.7sec	1/3sec	1/6sec	1/10sec	1/20sec	1/45sec	1/90sec	1/180sec	1/350sec	1/750sec	1/1500sec	1/3000sec	

UNDERSTANDING APERTURE SETTINGS

The illustration below shows the iris at one-stop increments, i.e. each step from left to right halves the amount of light passing through the lens. The maximum aperture setting refers to the iris wide open (in this instance f/2.8) and the minimum aperture is the iris at its smallest setting (f/32 in this case). An explanation of where the f/number derives from would require an extensive scientific explanation, but the key to you understanding apertures is to learn how f/numbers correlate with the size of the aperture.

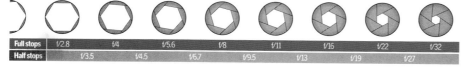

Full stops	f/2.8	f/4	f/5.6	f/8	f/11	f/16	f/22	f/32
Half stops	f/3.5	f/4.5	f/6.7	f/9.5	f/13	f/19	f/27	

Perfect exposure
Learning the basics of exposure
is key to ensuring your portraits
have the perfect combination of
shutter speed and aperture.

Understanding your DSLR's metering system

Before looking at how you can influence the exposure, it's best to understand how your camera's metering works. Here we've covered the essentials that you need to know in order to pick the best metering mode for different shooting conditions

DIGITAL SLRS BOAST complex exposure systems and offer a choice of metering patterns, each working out the exposure in a different way to suit varying lighting conditions. A camera's exposure system works on the assumption that the area of the scene that is being metered is a mid-tone, or 18% grey to be exact; the average if all dark, lights and mid-tones were mixed together. It's a tried and tested method and the basis of all metering patterns. It's important to be aware of this when you're taking pictures (even if you don't fully understand it) as it helps you to know when you may have problems with exposure.

While this system is fine in the majority of shooting situations, it can lead to incorrect exposures when the scene or subject is considerably lighter or darker in tone than 18% grey. For example, very dark subjects or scenes can fool the metering system into thinking that the general scene is much darker than it really is and, as a result, will overexposed the image. Similarly, very light subjects or scenes can fool the camera into underexposing them – making them appear darker than they are – as the light meter will take a reading designed to render them as a mid-tone. It's in these trickier lighting situations, where the popular multi-zone pattern that provides the correct exposure for around 90 percent of shots struggles as it tries to meter the entire scene. It's in cases like this where using the other patterns such as partial and spot are useful as they offer more control.

As a camera is trying to render an image grey, it's your job to ensure you compensate to keep the tones true to life. To do this you have to either overexpose the camera's reading to give a lighter result than the camera wants, or underexpose to give a darker result than the camera wants. So with a portrait in a dark scene, the camera's exposure reading will lead to overexposure, resulting in bleached faces, so you need to reduce the exposure to keep it black. With the light scene it's giving less exposure than is necessary, producing a darker than required subject, so you need to add exposure to make it record correctly. If you're still a little unsure, don't worry, when you start shooting light or dark scenes and then try to override the camera's readings, you'll soon get to grips with it. By following our expert advice you should also increase the chances of keeping any exposure errors to a minimum.

Multi-zone metering

In theory, you could take every picture using multi-zone metering and never have a bad exposure. Well almost... The multi-zone pattern is the newest and most sophisticated type of metering pattern and the one most photographers stick to for the majority of their shots. While every manufacturer has their own types of multi-zone meter, each with varying numbers and shapes of zones, all work in much the same way. Basically, the entire image area is divided into a number of zones and when activated, individual meter readings are taken from each one of them. The camera's micro-processor then evaluates all these individual readings and uses complex algorithms to calculate the final exposure. To improve accuracy, many cameras also boast a library of tens of thousands of images taken in various lighting conditions, which are compared in a micro-second with the new scene to produce the exposure value. This system has proven highly reliable and gets the exposure correct more than 90 percent of the time. Its weak spots however, are unusually light or very dark scenes or subjects. Multi-zone meters can also have trouble with very high-contrast scenes, in particular backlit subjects. This is why there are other metering patterns available, as well as a choice of exposure overrides, to help you ensure the perfect exposure.

Recognising the multi-zone pattern icon

Every camera brand has their own set of icons for metering patterns and below we show you what to look for on four popular brands

How to choose metering patterns

Selecting a metering pattern is a straightforward procedure, but we've provided a guide on how to do it for a number of leading digital SLRs from the six most popular brands

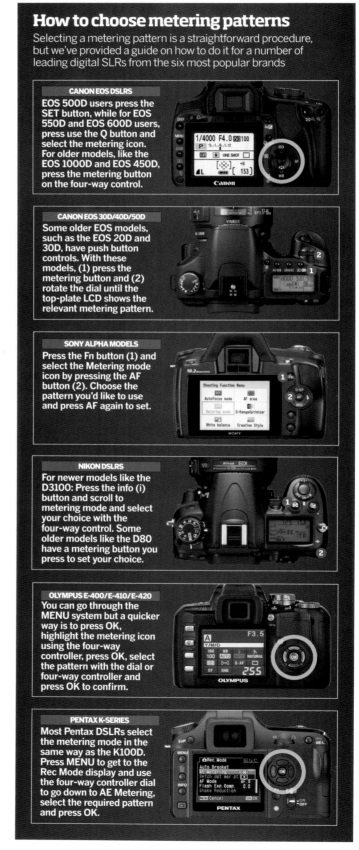

CANON EOS DSLRS
EOS 500D users press the SET button, while for EOS 550D and EOS 600D users, press use the Q button and select the metering icon. For older models, like the EOS 1000D and EOS 450D, press the metering button on the four-way control.

CANON EOS 30D/40D/50D
Some older EOS models, such as the EOS 20D and 30D, have push button controls. With these models, (1) press the metering button and (2) rotate the dial until the top-plate LCD shows the relevant metering pattern.

SONY ALPHA MODELS
Press the Fn button (1) and select the Metering mode icon by pressing the AF button (2). Choose the pattern you'd like to use and press AF again to set.

NIKON DSLRS
For newer models like the D3100: Press the info (i) button and scroll to metering mode and select your choice with the four-way control. Some older models like the D80 have a metering button you press to set your choice.

OLYMPUS E-400/E-410/E-420
You can go through the MENU system but a quicker way is to press OK, highlight the metering icon using the four-way controller, press OK, select the pattern with the dial or four-way controller and press OK to confirm.

PENTAX K-SERIES
Most Pentax DSLRs select the metering mode in the same way as the K100D. Press MENU to get to the Rec Mode display and use the four-way controller dial to go down to AE Metering, select the required pattern and press OK.

BJORN THOMASSEN

Metering options
Understanding how metering patterns work can help you when shooting in tricky lighting conditions, such as backlighting.

Centre-weighted average

Despite the arrival of newer patterns, this veteran still has its place on digital SLRs. This is the oldest metering pattern and was the number one choice until the multi-zone pattern was introduced. As its name suggests, it takes an average reading from the entire frame, with a slight emphasis given to the central area. While less sophisticated compared to newer patterns, its past popularity means it is still featured in all cameras, as many experienced photographers feel more comfortable using this pattern. It is also a good choice when used in combination with the AE-Lock exposure override, which is covered in more detail shortly.

Recognising the centre-weighted icon
You will find the centre-weighted pattern available on your DSLR but you will rarely need to have to use it in preference to multi-zone metering

Spot and partial metering

This is a great pattern when you want to take a reading from a specific area of the frame – but it must be used with care. While multi-zone metering takes measurements from the entire image area, spot and partial metering concentrates on the central area of the frame (you can see the measuring circle at the centre of the viewfinder screen). This allows you to precisely control where the exposure reading for the shot is taken from, as only the area of the frame within the measuring circle is used to determine the exposure. Spot and partial metering is a great way to ensure you get the proper exposure when you're shooting in difficult lighting conditions. Spot and partial are very similar in how they work. The main difference is spot offers a very precise measuring circle (usually around 3% of the image area), while partial usually measures the central 9% of the frame. The more precise spot meter is found on most DSLRs, while partial is less common, and a handful of cameras boast both. You must take great care when using spot or partial metering: always take a reading from a mid-tone and not a light or dark subject, otherwise you will produce an incorrect exposure.

Recognising the spot/partial icon
You need to select spot or partial by pressing the metering selector button and picking the respective icon on the LCD monitor. The spot icon is normally shown as a single dot at the centre of the rectangle, while partial is represented as two small curved lines that form the outline of a near-circle close to the centre of the frame. Some DSLRs offer both metering options.

CANON (PARTIAL)

REMEMBER: It's vital that you position the spot/partial meter over a mid-tone to get the correct exposure. Spot-meter off a dark subject and you'll overexpose it and vice-versa. Try some practice shots to get used to how it works.

Exposure compensation

This is the most commonly used override and allows you to make adjustments to increase or decrease the exposure

ONCE YOU ARE aware of how metering systems work, and have gained a little experience using your DSLR, the times when the exposure system is likely to make mistakes become easier to predict and compensate for. The simplest way to override your camera's metered exposure is to use exposure compensation, which allows you to dial in a set exposure increment to increase (+) or decrease (–) the exposure. For instance, a subject that is significantly lighter than a mid-tone, like a bride's white wedding dress, is likely to be underexposed by your camera, so you need to select positive (+) compensation. If the subject is much darker than a mid-tone, for instance the subject is wearing very dark clothing, then it is likely to be rendered overexposed. Therefore, apply negative (–) compensation. Applying exposure compensation is quite straightforward and with experience you'll be able to judge how much is needed. All digital SLRs have a dedicated exposure compensation button to make it a quick and easy process in either automatic or semi-automatic exposure modes. The compensation you set is often shown as + or – E.V (Exposure Value). If you add a half-stop of exposure it will display as +1/2EV, while a 1/3-stop reduction is shown as -1/3EV.

+1.5EV

-1.5EV

How does exposure compensation work?

Exposure compensation functions differently depending on the exposure mode that you are using. In aperture-priority, the compensation is applied by changing the shutter speed, but when using shutter-priority, it's the aperture that's adjusted. In program mode, the camera automatically decides between the aperture and/or shutter speed depending on the light levels so to minimise camera shake.

No compensation

+1 EV applied

EXPOSURE COMPENSATION
This is a typical example of when a subject deceives a metering system. When photographing this scene, the camera attempted to record it as a mid-tone and the first result was underexposed. Positive compensation of +1EV was applied, rendering the subjects in the subsequent image to be correctly exposed.

SUMMARY: EXPOSURE COMPENSATION
Set a + value to add exposure to an underexposed scene, for example when shooting a light-toned subject.
Set a - value to reduce the exposure, for example when shooting a darker than average scene.

Using exposure compensation

Your DSLR's exposure compensation facility is useful in any situation when you wish to make a picture brighter/lighter or darker than the exposure set by the camera. While exposure compensation is designed for corrective purposes, the effect can be used creatively. It's extremely easy to use: try applying '+' and '–' settings on subjects with different tones and see the effect it has. Here's how to do it:

1) Press and hold in your camera's exposure compensation button (normally indicated by a +/- icon).
2) Rotate the input dial to select the level of compensation you want. A negative value means you're decreasing the exposure, a positive value means you are increasing it.
3) The exposure compensation scale is displayed in the camera's viewfinder and/or control panel.
4) The compensation you apply will affect all subsequent shots unless you reset it to +/- 0 EV.

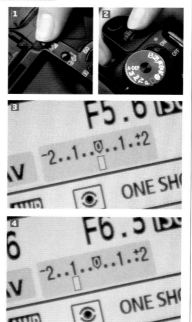

Auto Exposure Lock (AE-L)

This function allows you to 'lock' an exposure from a subject independently of the focusing system and is useful to avoid exposure error with very dark or light subjects or scenes

AE-Lock

AE-L PRACTICALLY EVERY DSLR has an AE-L button, which is normally found on the top right of the camera's rear, or near the LCD monitor. AE-L is an abbreviation for Auto Exposure Lock. It is designed to secure the current exposure setting so that it doesn't change when you recompose your image, even if the incoming light levels change. AE-L can be used in any exposure mode, although it is pointless if you are shooting in manual mode.

When you press the shutter button down halfway, you engage the autofocus and the metering system to take a reading. This is ideal most of the time, but what about when you want to focus and meter from different subjects or parts of the scene? This is where AE-Lock comes in. This useful feature allows you to take an exposure reading independently of where you focus, which is ideal if your subject is very dark or light or positioned in a bright or dim area of the scene. AE-L is most commonly used with the spot or centre-weighted metering pattern in order to 'lock' the reading taken from a specific area of the frame. This is particularly useful in tricky lighting conditions that can fool your metering system, such as backlit objects or subjects with very dark or light backgrounds. For instance, if you are shooting a scene containing a bright light source in part of the frame, your camera's multi-zone meter could be fooled by into reading the scene as brighter than it actually is and will underexpose as a result. To achieve the correct exposure, you want to take a meter reading that excludes the light region. This is possible by taking a spot/partial meter reading from the subject itself or an area of the scene that is a mid-tone and locking the result with the AE-Lock button, before recomposing the shot and taking the picture. Using the same principle, AE-L is useful when shooting subjects that are positioned off-centre. AE-Lock is also useful when you want to shoot a series of images using exactly the same exposure settings. For example, if you wish to stitch together several shots to create a panorama, it is important that the shooting parameters employed for each frame are consistent – using the AE-Lock button ensure contant exposures for each shot.

The AE-Lock button is an essential exposure aid when shooting subjects with very dark or light backgrounds that can easily fool your camera's multi-zone metering into over or underexpose. In this instance, the very dark backdrop fooled the camera into thinking the scene was darker than it actually was. As a result, it has set a shutter speed longer than was required and so the subject is overexposed. In order to achieve the correct exposure, a spot-meter reading was taken from a wall to the side of the stairs. This reading was then locked using the AE-Lock button. The image was recomposed and the image taken. The result is perfectly exposed.

Using AE-Lock

The AE-L button, combined with spot or centre-weighted metering, is one of the most accurate forms of achieving the correct exposure settings for any given subject.

1) Select your camera's spot (or partial) meter.

2) Direct the camera so that the metering circle is positioned over the area or subject that you wish to meter from.

3) Activate AE-Lock by pressing the button. Note: on some models you have to keep it depressed, so consult your user's manual. The letters 'AE-L' may display in the viewfinder to indicate the lock is activated.

4) Move the camera and recompose the image as you want. Your exposure settings will not change, even if the incoming light levels alter as a result of changing composition.

6) Fully depress the shutter release button to take the shot.

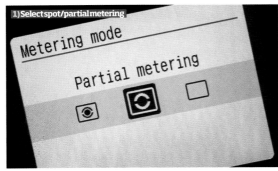

1) Select spot/partial metering

Metering mode

Partial metering

3) Use AE-Lock

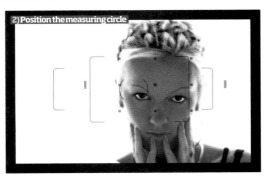

2) Position the measuring circle

4) Recompose and shoot

Exposing backlit subjects

Paul Stefan shows you to how to perfectly exposure a backlit portrait using the spot meter, a reflector and a bit of fill-in flash

SHOOTING A BACKLIT subject (i.e. with the sun behind them) is not something I do too often, as it certainly comes with its challenges. If you're not prepared for it, your results can often be quite unpredictable and, more often than not, your subject will be underexposed and look rather flat. This tutorial will help you to understand the relatively straightforward technique to achieving great results.

Let's begin with why letting the camera make the decisions for you is not the best option. It's often so easy to stick your camera on Full Auto mode and let it decide the exposure. For portraits that have the light shining on the subject's face, or off slightly to the side, using auto mode sometimes works fine, as the exposure levels may not be too extreme. However, if you position your subject so that the light source is behind them (so you're shooting towards them and the sun or light source), your

camera is likely to get confused and the exposure terribly wrong. What usually happens is your subject gets underexposed, sometimes silhouetted, often resulting in an awful picture. The reason for this is that the camera's multi-zone exposure system will evaluate the overall scene. Given that you are pointing the camera towards the light source, it will always look to expose the shot for a bright scene, causing the darker areas – in this case the person – to be underexposed.

Taking more control over your camera will greatly improve the image and enable you to get the exposure you really want. One of the easiest ways to do this is to set your DSLR to aperture-priority mode and to use the spot meter along with AE-Lock to fix the light reading. With this method, you take a spot meter reading from the person's face, regardless of the lighting conditions around the subject, which should result in a perfectly-exposed person nearly

every time. The exception, when it might be slightly trickier, is when your subject is very dark-skinned. If that's the case, use the same technique but take a spot meter reading off a mid-tone in the same lighting conditions, this could be a piece of clothing, grass or ideally an 18% grey card.

While spot metering is quick and easy, it may cause your subject's surrounding scene to be overexposed if it's lighter than your subject. If you want to include the environment in the shot, one way around this is to take a meter reading from an in-between subject and then use your camera's flash to fill in the foreground with light, balancing the overall scene's exposure. Equally, a reflector will also help this, as it will bounce natural light back towards your subject and have a similar fill-in effect. If you're feeling really adventurous, why not try a mixture, using both flash and a reflector.

Try spot in manual
You can use the spot meter in manual mode. Change apertures and shutter speeds until the exposure scale reaches the correct setting. This saves you having to use the AE-Lock function

1) Take a shot with your DSLR set to Full Auto
I was keen for my portrait to have a picturesque backdrop, so I chose a south-facing hillside near my home, with a view looking out to Robin Hood's Stride and Cratcliffe in the Peak District. My first shot was to see how the camera's Auto mode handled the exposure of my subject with the sun directly behind and above her. With this set up, I was shooting towards the sun, which would certainly challenge the camera's multi-zone metering system.

2) Using spot metering and a reflector
The shot taken in Full Auto wasn't a disaster, but it could certainly be improved with the use of spot metering. By switching my DSLR to aperture-priority and setting the metering mode to spot, I was able to meter from Emily's face and lock the reading using AE-Lock. I did this by looking through the viewfinder and placing the central circle over the her face and pressing the AE-Lock button to ensure a perfect exposure. I then focused on her face, recomposed and took the shot.

The result from my DSLR wasn't actually too bad as the face of my subject, my eldest daughter Emily, wasn't completely underexposed, but it could definitely be improved. This would have been much worse if the sun was lower and in direct view of the shot. Other DSLRs may not have coped as well as my Canon EOS 5D MkII either.

Spot metering has improved the scene greatly, but to make it even better, I placed a portable reflector just out of shot, perched on a stick, to throw some of that lovely warm sunlight back onto Emily's face, giving the shot added depth. This really made a difference, revealing so much more detail and depth, both in her face and in her clothes.

3) Use fill-in flash

I like the natural look of the spot-metered and reflector shot, but for this example I wanted to show a further change to the set-up, to create a more dramatic portrait. Therefore, I hooked up my flashgun to my camera with a stretchy sync lead, to allow me to hold the flash unit away from the camera and over to one side. This is a useful technique that causes your flash to give a more flattering look to the subject, rather than blasting them directly in the face. With this set-up, I also left the reflector in place, used the same exposure settings from the previous shot and pointed the flashgun toward Emily's body, rather than her face.

The flash has made quite an impact on how she's lit. Her face is a lot brighter, but because I aimed the flashgun towards her body and feet, the shot has exposed her lower half so much better than the previous shot. Her hair is also really well exposed and she now has catchlights in her eyes from the flash.

240-4788 ISO100 sRGB

1/200 5.0 Av RAW+4L 5.84MB 13/04/2009 16:08:41 176/274

Portrait composition

There are no rules, only guidelines when it comes to composition but, like lighting, it has the potential to make or break a portrait. Developing your style will take time and practice but here are a few of the main considerations to take into account and to help you along your way

1) Landscape or upright orientation?

It's natural to tilt the camera upright when you're shooting a portrait as it allows you to fill the frame with the subject's head and shoulders or entire body. It's a good format to adopt when you're trying to exclude as much of the background as possible to concentrate attention on the subject. Because this format is used so often when shooting people, the upright format is often termed the portrait format. Photographing portraits with the camera held normally to produce a landscape-orientated image often allows you to employ more creative compositions. For one, it means you can place the subject off-centre to include some of the backdrop in the frame. It also allows you to crop tightly into the face, which can add drama and impact to the image. Both options are worth trying while looking through the viewfinder to see which works best and, if in doubt, take a shot using both formats!

We have cropped the same image (see right) into a landscape and portrait format. Which do you prefer? The orientation you opt for plays a crucial role in the strength of your portrait and it's a choice you need to make each time you compose a shot.

Landscape

Portrait

2) Viewpoint

It's natural when taking a picture to stand and shoot from your normal eye-level. However, while there is nothing wrong with this, shooting from your standard viewpoint is a little unimaginative. Also, it's not always the most flattering angle for your subject – you'll find that by shooting from slightly above and down on your subject, you'll capture a better picture. Experiment by shooting from a much higher or lower viewpoint to your subject and see how the results turn out.

Shooting a subject from halfway up some steps provides a very high viewpoint and produces an unusual and quirky result. Give it a try!

3) Breaking the rules: New angles to try

USE A WIDE-ANGLE LENS
Set your standard zoom to wide-angle (or use an ultra wide-angle zoom) and shoot portraits with a difference. Because they completely distort perspective, it's possible to shoot very unusual portrait images, where the part of the subject closest to the lens appears much larger than the parts of the body that are further away.

EYE CONTACT
Yep, we harp on about making sure you get both eyes sharply in focus with the subject looking at the camera, yet there are many stunning examples where the subject's looking away or their eyes are obscured. A lack of eye contact can add intrigue to your portrait or give it a candid feel, so don't be afraid of having your subject looking away from the camera.

Look how the wide-angle lens used on this shot has distorted perspective. You can get some quirky portraits from using unconventional techniques.

✓ **Location, location**
Virtually any location is suitable for taking portraits. You'll find you can take great portraits anywhere as long as you use the light correctly. Make it a project to walk around your local neighbourhood trying to spot decent backdrops

Shoot on a slant
Shooting images at an angle can add energy to an image as it displaces the balance of the scene. Give it a try, whether shooting with the camera in an upright or landscape format, and see how it can inject life into the image.

Frequently asked questions

My camera has scene modes, why should I not use Portrait mode?
While it takes the fuss out of taking a picture, Portrait mode removes any chance of being creative. As with all scene modes, the Portrait program automatically activates certain picture-taking options. Depending on which camera you use, you'll find that setting Portrait mode results in the following: *White Balance: Auto; Autofocus: Multi-point AF/One-shot mode; ISO Rating: Automatically selected; Metering pattern: Multi-zone; Built-in flash: Auto.*

While these settings are suitable for those looking for point-and-shoot simplicity, for those of you wanting to develop your photographic skills, it's quite prohibitive and the fact that you can't control aspects such as the flash and White Balance can really affect the result you're trying to achieve. Instead, learn how to get the best from semi-automatic modes such as aperture-priority.

What should subjects wear?
The most important thing is that your subject feels comfortable. So don't get them to overdress or wear items that they don't like.

Ideally, ask to see a selection of clothing and talk through what they like the most. You don't want colours to dominate the image, so a plain neutral top is usually a good starting point, along with casual trousers or a pair of jeans.

How should I get them to pose?
It's vital that they appear natural and comfortable, whether they're sitting, standing or lying down. You'll find that subjects are normally unsure of what to do with their hands, resulting in them looking clumsy or awkward in the frame. A good starting point is to have them keep their hands in their trouser pockets if standing, hanging over their knees or between their legs if sat down. Buy fashion and lifestyle magazines and tear out

pages where a model has a pose you like, then show it to your subject and ask them to recreate it.

Have you got any make-up tips?
We asked professional make-up artist Fay Bacon for expert advice:
1) Always thoroughly cleanse, tone and moisturise the skin before applying any make-up. It will help the products to sit better on the skin.
2) Apply an illuminator over the top of a moisturiser. This helps lift the skin and increase its radiance underneath the foundation, so skin appears more youthful.
3) Always apply foundation with a foundation brush as it reduces the amount of foundation used on the skin and prevents patchiness or lines on the face, making the skin appear extra-flawless and natural.
4) Use a translucent, loose powder and dust it lightly over the 'T-Zone' area. This reduces the appearance of shiny, oily skin.

5) Always use concealer for disguising dark circles and unwanted blemishes. There is an enormous difference between foundation and concealer; foundation evens out the skin tone while concealer covers. You need to use both to achieve flawless-looking skin.
6) In terms of colour such as eye shadows, blushers and lipsticks etc, always consider the colour contrasts of skin tone, eyes and lips. Dependent upon the style and theme of the photography shoot certain make-up rules do not apply. However, most make-up artists would advise using lighter and more intense shades such as purples, blues and greens on darker skin and eyes, as this helps echo the beauty and vibrancy of the skin tone.

Pastel, neutral and darker shades are better suited for paler skin as they help intensify the eye area and the skin tone by allowing both to stand out more.

Put the 'rules' into practice

Set-up

Taking photographs of people is something that nearly everyone with a camera does. Whether it be a friend, a family member or a professional model, it's often easy to snap away at a person and end up with, well... a snapshot. A little bit of consideration for composition, however, will go a long way to improving your portraits and hopefully capture your subject's personality better too.

The standard rules of composition remain the same for portraits as they do for most photographs. The rule-of-thirds, filling the frame and thinking about your setting/background are all factors that will drastically improve a portrait and ultimately determine its success. If used correctly and creatively, these guidelines will help convert your photographs from snapshots to pictures to be proud of. In the next few steps, we'll show what the difference applying these rules can have on your photographs.

Step 1 This first shot is an example of what not to do. Without considering the rules of composition, you may end up with a nice enough snapshot, but the main focal point (the eyes) aren't in a third, making the composition look awkward. In addition, the building work in the background is distracting for the viewer and the green trees sticking out of the subject's head don't look good. As a beginner, thinking about the background is definitely one of the easiest ways to improve the composition of your portraits quickly.

Left: Step 2 As all Rocky Horror fans will say: "It's just a jump to the left!" In the next shot, the subject was asked to take one step to her left, this immediately improved composition by incorporating a much simpler backdrop. Compared to the first image, you can immediately see the improvement it's made to the overall impact of the picture. The texture and tone is much simpler, keeping the viewer's eye focused on the model's face.

Above: Step 3 The placement of the eyes within the frame is paramount to improving composition. Generally, a portrait works best if the eyes are in the top third of the shot, as it guides the viewer from top to bottom. Getting a bit closer and using a 70mm focal length, as opposed to the 50mm used in the previous two shots, has meant the subject now fills the frame with more of the her face. Getting closer also helps blur the background more.

Final image
The shot could still be improved by tweaking the composition in a couple of ways. Here the frame has been filled even more with a subject's face to create a more intimate portrait. The focal points (eyes and hair band) have also been moved to the upper left third and shot at an angle for a more dynamic look. A wider aperture of f/6.3 has also completely blurred the background for a more pleasing result.

Breaking rules is child's play!

APPLYING THE RULES of composition to portraits, such as the placement of the eyes in the upper third and using diagonals and lead-in lines, are great ways of improving your portrait photographs. But as you'll no doubt have discovered, sometimes rules are there to be broken, and when it comes to the composition of portraits, breaking these rules can lead to some quirky results.

This step-by-step guide aims to show you how to shoot portraits with a difference. Instead of using a typical portrait lens like a 50mm, we've opted to use a 17-40mm wide-angle zoom at its widest focal length. This type of lens can often be very unflattering for a portrait, as your model can end up with distorted features, so composition becomes even more important! You should still pay particular attention to elements such as the rule-of-thirds, your subject's background and so on, but don't be afraid to consider these more as guidelines than rules. You should look for unconventional ways of approaching a portrait, bending the rules a little to get a more unusual and creative portrait.

Set-up

Step 1 This first shot, using the zoom set at 17mm, gives a very distorted view of the subject and is a good example of how not to bend the rules. Little thought has been given to the positioning of the eyes, which is usually the focal point, so they have ended up in the centre of the frame. Nor has much attention been paid to what's going on with the background and surroundings. The slightly quirky angle has also made the composition a little too awkward, although the lead-in lines of the legs work well. Breaking the compositional rules in this shot hasn't worked out as well as it should have and can certainly be improved.

Left: Step 2 For the second shot, the focal length was kept at 17mm and the model has turned around for a more frame-filling shot. Although the model's eyes aren't on a third, which could improve the image, having the lead-in line created by the elbow from the bottom left does work better than the previous shot. Typically in a portrait you wouldn't want your model to have tiny feet but breaking this rule gives the shot an interesting perspective.

Above: Step 3 This shot has challenged the rules of focusing, and it works well. Instead of concentrating on the subject's eyes, the focus is on the leaves in her hand. Using an aperture of f/4 has meant her face is blurred, which is not something you would usually want to do with a portrait. This has made the image more intriguing and with a wider angle, I've been able to place the two main subjects of the shot at the top and the bottom of the image.

Final image

This shot combines all the best elements of the other images. Using the wide-angle lens, the model was shot from above with an aperture of f/4. The eye remains the focal point and the background texture has been simplified with a single texture, so it enhances rather than distracts. The quirky angle and unconventional crop works well with this shot too.

Focusing fundamentals

While the autofocus systems of digital SLRs are highly responsive, we can help to improve their accuracy

AUTOFOCUS IS ONE OF THOSE THINGS that all photographers take for granted at one time or another. Half-press the shutter release and it does its job quickly and quietly. While everything is working well, you don't really need to think about what's happening and why, but taking control of the autofocus (AF) can help you improve, especially when your DSLR struggles to interpret what you are trying to do. Understanding how this highly advanced technology works will ultimately help you to use it more effectively in your photography.

HOW AUTOFOCUS SYSTEMS WORK

There are two main kinds of autofocus system used in modern cameras: contrast detection AF and phase detection AF. In DSLRs, the latter of these is used most of the time. Phase detection AF works by taking some of the light entering the camera through the lens, splitting it into two and directing it onto a pair of sensors. The point where it hits the sensors tells the camera if the image is in focus or not, and if not by how much it's out and in what direction. This means that the camera can find the correct focus very quickly. The downside of phase detection AF is that it needs contrast in order to work. Point your camera at a blank wall and the system simply won't function.

Phase detection AF also requires a DSLR's mirror to be down, meaning it doesn't work so well in Live View mode. This is when we need contrast detection AF – the same system that is used in compact cameras. It works by continuously monitoring the overall contrast in a scene while focusing, the idea being that an image has the most contrast when it's at its sharpest. It's a slower method, suited to tripod-mounted work where speed isn't so important.

AUTOFOCUS MODES

DSLRs have two popular AF modes. The first, and perhaps the most useful, is Single-Shot AF (know as One-Shot on Canon EOS DSLRs). In this mode, you typically press halfway down on your camera's shutter release to engage AF. Once this has happened, focus is locked at this distance until you release the button and half-press it again. Single-Shot AF mode also prevents the shutter firing unless the subject is in focus. Continuous autofocus mode, on the other hand, will let the shutter fire at any point regardless of whether the scene is in focus or not, and will carry on focusing even when your finger is half-pressing the shutter button. It's the mode best suited to photographing moving subjects, as we'll see shortly. While we are on the subject of focus modes, it's worth mentioning good-old manual mode too. There are times when autofocus is simply not the best option, and focusing manually produces better results, such as with night photography, where low light confuses AF, and macro, where focusing is so critical that it is often best to focus manually.

MULTI-POINT AUTOFOCUS

Early AF systems used a single sensor at the centre of the frame. DSLRs now have multiple AF points grouped centrally and occupying up to half the frame. The advantage of this is that you're not limited to focusing on whatever is in the middle of a scene, allowing the AF system to comfortably handle off-centre subjects or objects that are moving around in the frame.

The most focusing points in a DSLR is currently 51 (Nikon) but the average is around 11. Shoot with all points activated and the camera will focus on what is closest to you – handy in most situations, but with portraits, can result in the lens focusing on the tip of the nose rather than the eyes. You usually have the option of reducing the number of active focus points, which increases focus speed precision and allows you to focus on a precise point.

Not all focus points are the same either, in fact there are two distinct types. Line-type sensors are the most common, but least sensitive. They are oriented in one direction only (usually top-to-bottom) and need to be looking at detail that crosses them perpendicularly (left-to-right) to focus accurately. Cross-type sensors look for detail in both directions, and are faster and more sensitive. The central focus point will usually be a cross-type sensor, though more advanced DSLRs often have a number of them clustered together.

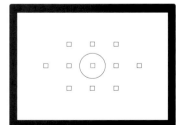

Select single-point AF and focus precisely on your chosen subject. Choosing the central point is usually best.

Multi-point AF

Multi-point AF activates all the sensors and usually focuses on whatever is closest to you. It's ideal for tracking subjects such as a child running.

Setting autofocus modes on your DSLR

Selecting the autofocus mode and the number of active AF points differs from camera to camera. Here's we show how it works on five popular models from the leading brands – you'll find your DSLR works in a similar way

CANON EOS (MOST MODELS)

AF MODE: Press the AF button (located on the right side of the four-way control) and choose from One Shot, AI Focus or AI Servo mode.

AF POINTS: Press the AF point selection button on the top right of the rear of the camera and use the input dial by the shutter release button to choose the AF point.

NIKON DSLRS

AF MODE: Press the info (i) button and scroll to Focus mode. Use the four-way control and OK button to select AF-A, AF-S, AF-C or manual focus.

AF POINTS: Press the info button and scroll down to the AF-area mode option. Choose between Closest Subject, Dynamic Area where you can select a focus point for tracking, or Single Point.

OLYMPUS E-SERIES

AF MODE: Press OK and scroll to the AF mode option. Press OK again and choose between S-AF (single-shot AF), C-AF (continuous AF) and MF (manual focus).

AF POINTS: Press OK and scroll to the AF Area option. You can then use the command dial to select all the AF points or select an individual point.

PENTAX K-SERIES

AF MODE: Press the MENU button and use the four way control to select AF Mode. AF.S is the single-shot AF mode, while AF.C is continuous AF mode.

AF POINTS: Press the MENU button and use the four-way control to go down to Select AF point. Choose from Auto, multi-point or spot AF (the camera uses the central AF point only.

SONY ALPHA SERIES

AF MODE: Press Fn and choose the Autofocus mode option using the four way control. Choose between AF-S AF-A or AF-C mode.

AF POINTS: Press the Fn button and then choose the AF area option using the four-way control. Choose between Wide (all points), Spot (centre point) and Local (manual selection of any AF point).

BRETT HARKNESS

Focus on off-centre subjects

WHEN YOU ARE OUT SHOOTING, it's not often that your subject will be slap-bang in the middle of the frame. In fact, we often go to great lengths when taking pictures to avoid placing the subject at the centre to ensure the image has the best possible composition.

If your DSLR has multiple focus points spread across a wide area then, chances are, these will manage off-centre subjects very well. For the ultimate control though, try selecting one individual AF point to take charge of exactly where your camera is focusing. The traditional way of handling off-centre subjects with a single focus point comprises three steps: using the central AF point to focus on the subject; locking the focus using your camera's AF-lock function; and recomposing the frame so that your subject is off-centre. Your DSLR's AF-lock is easy to find. Providing your camera is set to Single-Shot AF mode, a half-press of the shutter release will tell the camera to focus and then lock-in this distance for as long as the button is held down. It's an intuitive process, you'll soon find yourself performing the focus-lock-recompose routine without realising it.

By default, on the majority of cameras, pressing the shutter button halfway not only locks the focus, but also takes an exposure reading too. Try it yourself and see how your DSLR performs. You'll find you can usually use a custom function to set the shutter release to lock AF and the exposure together, or just the AF. Some DSLRs have a separate AF/AE-lock button, meaning it's possible to customise the AF so it's just the way you like it.

Use depth-of-field to give your portraits much more impact

By altering your shooting distance, being creative with your focusing and thinking about your choice of aperture, you stand a great chance of make your portraits outstanding

THERE ARE FEW, IF ANY, MORE rewarding feelings in photography than capturing a portrait that not only pleases you, but has the subject over the moon with how they look in the shot. Most people have had their picture taken, but few get the chance to have their portrait shot. There is a subtle difference to the two: one is a quick snap, with little attention given to anything but basic composition and the other is far more creative and carefully considered.

It's often said that a good portrait captures a little bit of the person's personality and it's true. But what it also does is record the sitter in a different way to other pictures taken of them. By using a couple of simple techniques based around depth-of-field and focusing, you can produce distinctive results, as you will discover shortly.

The general rule for portraits is that you should focus on the eyes and set a wide aperture (usually at least f/5.6) to throw the background out of focus, while keeping the face sharp. The 'f/5.6 rule' is one that is used frequently and successfully by many professional lifestyle photographers, who like to work fast and prefer to concentrate on their interaction with the subject rather than changing settings. If you want to include more of the environment, however, in the frame, a smaller aperture (usually coupled with a wider lens) is required to keep the background, as well as the subject, in sharp focus.

While ambient light is quite often sufficient – and sometimes ideal – you should also consider using studioflash. As well as allowing you to control the direction of the light, you can adjust the intensity to provide the exact amount of light you need for any given aperture. Once you learn how to use it correctly, a one or two-light set-up can also open up scope for creative opportunities.

Portraits can look exceptionally flattering when the zone of sharpness is extremely shallow. The easiest way to do this is to follow all the 'tricks' that are required to give an image the shallowest depth-of-field, namely using a telezoom set to the maximum aperture with a relatively short shooting distance. The result is a tight crop of the face where, bar a small focused area, much of the frame is thrown out of focus. The result is a very 'soft' image that, with some thought given to lighting, can look romantic if lit by diffused light, or more arty and striking if used with

f/5.6 at 200mm

f/5.6 at 200mm

SHOOTING DISTANCE
Both shots were taken using the same lens and aperture, but depth-of-field was altered by changing the shooting distance. The shorter distance gives less depth-of-field, which blurs the window blinds.

strong directional light. When using this technique, be sure to focus on the appropriate part of the face, usually an eye but sometimes the mouth, depending on where you want the viewer's gaze drawn to. It's certainly worth giving it a go with a friend or family member and seeing how you get on.

Portrait top tips

1) SHOOT HANDHELD It will enable you to move more freely and frame quicker. Better still, use a monopod. Using the maximum aperture provides the fastest possible shutter speed, but if it's still low, use the image stabiliser if your DSLR or lens has it and/or raise the ISO rating.

2) CHECK YOUR DISTANCE At very wide apertures, you have to be careful not to move forward or backward after focusing as this will lead to an unsharp shot.

3) EYE CONTACT Ensure that the subject's eyes are clean and make-up has been carefully applied. Try some shots with the subject looking into the lens and others with them looking away.

4) USE THE SHADOWS Pay attention to the lighting and to where the shadows fall, as they can add drama to an image.

5) CONSIDER MONO It's always worth converting portraits to black & white and seeing how they compare to colour images.

Differential focusing

Another popular technique when using shallow depth-of-field is differential focusing. It's a simple one to master but the secret is knowing when to use it. The basic principle is to use a very wide aperture to emphasise a particular subject within the frame by having it in focus while the rest of the scene (background or foreground) is out of focus. It's particularly effective when there is a lot of depth in the scene and you're using a wide aperture that blurs elements in the frame to the point that it's still recognisable. Use it to pick out a particular person in a crowd or to produce a creative portrait with a story to tell.

HIDE AND SEEK: These images illustrate the effect differential focusing has on an image. The same exposure was used in both shots but the focus was changed to reveal different elements in the scene.

Focus on nearest person

Focus on furthest person

Creative use of depth-of-field
Depth-of-field is one of the most creative in-camera tools, so think how you can use it to add an extra dimension to your images.

PORTRAIT LIGHTING

ESSENTIAL ADVICE & TECHNIQUES THAT WILL HELP YOU TO CONTROL LIGHT LIKE A PRO

How to control daylight

Understanding how to manipulate available light is an essential skill for the portrait photographer to master

WORKING WITH DAYLIGHT has several advantages and disadvantages for the portrait photographer compared to artificial light sources such as studioflash and flashguns. Daylight is incredibly versatile: the range of images that are possible, depending on the weather and the time of day, and the wide variety of lighting effects are tremendous. And, lets not forget it's free! However, unfortunately, available light – as it's often termed – has the problem of also being unavailable – both at night or on days of particularly poor weather when light levels are too low to justify the effort. One of the most wonderful things about working with daylight is that it allows you the chance to shoot outdoors in literally any location. Whether it's in the local park, a scrapyard or down by the coast, the options for great daylight portraits are limited only by your imagination and the ability you have to control daylight. And in the respect of the latter, despite the light source being millions of miles away, you still have plenty of control over how daylight falls on the subject, simply through the use of basic lighting aids such as reflectors and diffusers. Over the course of the following pages we'll show you how using the most basic of lighting accessories and techniques can transform your daylight portraits. As you'll discover, compared to shooting a straightforward snap, the extra effort required to place your subject correctly and use a lighting aid is minimal, but the difference it makes to the final images will be evident. So invest in a reflector or two and, should you be really keen on shooting outdoor portraits, buy a diffuser too, they'll really help to improve your portrait pictures.

Setting up your DSLR for daylight portraits

EXPOSURE Before you head outdoors, take a minute to prepare your DSLR so once you're on location, you can begin shooting without delay. Firstly, you should set your camera to aperture-priority mode, as you'll want to ensure that the depth-of-field is limited. We'd recommend you start by shooting at f/5.6. If shutter speeds are low enough to risk shake, raise the ISO rating to 400 and switch on image stabilisation if you have it.

METERING In terms of metering, you should find the multi-zone pattern to be perfectly adequate, but if you're shooting a dark-skinned person close-up, be prepared to add one to two stops exposure compensation.

FOCUSING We'd suggest you switch from multi-point AF to central-point focus as otherwise you risk focusing on the subject's brows or nose, rather than the eyes. Point the central AF point over the eye and half-depress the shutter button to lock focus, then recompose and shoot.

ALSO CONSIDER... While you can shoot with the White Balance set to Auto (AWB), you're better off setting it once you've arrived at the scene to the most suitable preset, especially if you're shooting in JPEG only. We'd strongly recommend you shoot in Raw + JPEG, though; this way you can review the smaller JPEG images on your computer. Then open and process your Raw files for ultimate quality, including any adjustments to White Balance or exposure that you need to make.

Which lens is best?

Using a telephoto focal length, which flattens perspective, is the best choice as it gives the most flattering portraits. You can get away with using the tele-end of your standard zoom, but you'll find a telephoto zoom, such as a 55-200mm, is a far better choice. Alternatively, you could go 'old-school' and shoot with a prime lens such as a 50mm f/1.8 (effectively an 80mm with APS-C sensors), which has the advantage of a wider maximum aperture than zooms.

Setting your DSLR for daylight portraits

Select aperture priority, set the White Balance for the shooting conditions and centre-point AF. You're now ready to shoot!

CANON EOS 500D/550D/600D

1) Set the mode dial on the top-plate to Av to select aperture-priority mode.

2) Press the WB button and use the four-way control to select White Balance. Select the WB preset you want to use and then press the OK button.

3) Press the AF points button and select central-point AF.

4) Press the AF button and set the AF mode to One Shot.

NIKON DSLRS INCLUDING D3100/5100

1) Set the mode dial on the right of the top-plate to A to select aperture-priority mode.

2) Press the i button and use the four-way control to select White Balance. Select the WB preset you want to use and then press the OK button.

Press i again and set the AF mode to AF-S and the AF-area mode to central-point only.

OLYMPUS E-SERIES

1) Set the mode dial on the right of the top-plate to A to select aperture-priority mode.

2) Press the OK button and use the four-way control to select White Balance. Select the WB preset you want to use and then press the OK button.

Press OK again and set the AF mode to S-AF and the AF points to central-point only.

PENTAX K-SERIES

1) Set the mode dial on the left of the top-plate to Av to select aperture-priority mode.

2) Press the OK button and use the four-way control to select White Balance. Select the WB preset you want to use and then press the OK button.

3) Press MENU, then select the Rec. Mode tab and set the AF mode to AF.S and then select the central AF point.

SONY ALPHA SERIES

1) Set the mode dial on the left of the top-plate to A to select aperture-priority mode.

2) Press the Fn button and use the four-way control to select White balance. Press the AF button and select the WB preset you want to use.

Now press the Fn button again, select Autofocus mode and select Spot in AF area and AF-S in Autofocus mode.

Shooting portraits with daylight is a great way to get to grips with the fundamental techniques of lighting and to learn how to use aids such as reflectors and diffusers.

Main lighting accessories for daylight portraits

When working with daylight, you don't have the level of control that studioflash allows with lighting direction and intensity. But while you can't control the sun itself, by using reflectors, diffusers or a combination of the two, you can control the amount of daylight reaching your subject. Reflectors and diffusers come in various forms, with the most common covered here.

REFLECTORS This simple accessory is incredibly effective at filling in shadows and can make a major improvement to your portraits. The standard type – and the one you should begin with – has a white side and a silver side (1). The white side reflects a clean, neutral light and is ideal when you can place it relatively close to the subject, as it reflects an even spread of light. The silver is far more efficient, producing a stronger result, so can be overpowering in bright sunlight or if placed too close to the subject, but is ideal in very overcast conditions or when shooting in shade. Gold reflectors are also available and like silver, are very efficient, but add a warm golden glow to the light. You should look for collapsible reflectors as they're light and easy to store away. The larger the reflector, the wider the area they cover –

look for a minimum diameter of 80cm and don't go too big as they can be cumbersome to use. Those with grips, such as Lastolite's Tri-Grip, are great when you have no assistance, as you can hold it with one hand. Other reflectors to check out are those that come with a silver and gold slip-on sleeve (2) or those with a lightweight frame, such as the California Sunbounce (3).

Controlling bright sunlight

A bright summer's day may seem like the ideal time to shoot outdoor portraits, but only if you know how to diffuse harsh directional sunlight to produce flattering results

THERE ARE MANY BENEFITS to taking photos outdoors on a day when the sky is blue and the sun is beaming. Light levels are very high, so you've a full range of apertures and shutter speeds to choose from, even with the ISO rating set to a low sensitivity for maximum image quality. Also, because the weather is warmer, subjects are happier to sit and pose for you and you've a full choice of outfits for them to wear. Plus, because the light is so bright, colours tend to be punchier and saturation higher, which all help add extra impact to images.

However, while there are many benefits to shooting in sunlight, there are also drawbacks to take into account. The first is the most obvious: sunlight is very bright and direct, so if your subject is facing it, they will most likely be squinting and their face and chin will have very harsh shadows, which amounts to a very unflattering portrait. Facing them away from the sun is one solution, but you'll then need to watch out for flare, as well as cope with a subject whose face is in deep shadow. The high contrast between the bright background and the subject also means that you'll have to be careful with metering, to ensure that the subject isn't underexposed.

The other solution, which we illustrate here, is to use a diffuser panel, placed between the sun and the subject, to bathe the model in a far more flattering light. In effect you're shading the subject from the sun, but using a diffuser offers a number of differences to placing the subject within a shaded location. The nature of light passing through a diffuser is very non-directional, much like shade, but because the light has passed through a white material, it's neutral, clean and retains a relatively high level of illumination. Whereas in the shade, the light is reflected off surfaces, which if coloured will influence the light falling on the subject. And, because the light has bounced off one or more surfaces, it will be less bright, meaning you have less choice with exposure settings.

The other key difference is that by diffusing direct sunlight, you're not limited in terms of location. You can shoot from the middle of a garden, beach or park, or anywhere else that suits your fancy, as you're able to use the diffuser panel to control the light falling on the subject. And as the diffused light is even, you can shoot from any direction, therefore being able to place the subject against a backdrop of your choice.

Shooting into light

If you don't have a diffuser, you can try shooting with the sun to your subject's back and try to find a position where the sun is obscured from view. Using the leaves of a tree is one option, or, as in this example, a wide-brimmed hat provides a very photogenic solution. Use a white reflector to bounce light back towards the subject and either use AE-Lock to take a reading from their face, or add between +1 to +2 stops of exposure compensation.

Sunlit step-by-step

For this simple step-by-step, we've taken some pictures in a garden using a Lastolite Skylite, which is a large diffuser panel that requires at least one person to hold it. Smaller panels that are easier to handhold are available but bear in mind that the diffused area will also be smaller. Take a look at the *Portrait Gear* section for further details of the types of diffusers available. As you'll see, reflectors also have their part to play in manipulating diffused light to help give the effect you're looking for. In this shoot, the camera was set to aperture-priority mode at f/5.6 (ISO 100) and White Balance to Sunlight.

1 Here's the basic set-up for the pictures. We're shooting around 3pm so the sun's still very high in the sky, so the diffuser has to be held over Ruby's head. You can see the large area of diffused light it produces beneath her.

2 This is the result of this basic set-up. Because the sun is obscured by the panel, Ruby isn't squinting and as the diffuser is just above her head, her hair has an attractive highlight. However, while the light on her face is fairly even, there are still some faint shadows that need removing.

3 To add a little colour to the diffused light, I place a sunfire reflector on the grass within the diffused shade, angled up towards Ruby's face. It's a powerful reflector, but as I'm positioned under the panel its effect doesn't cause Ruby to squint.

4 The resulting image is much better than the shot captured using the diffuser alone. The light from the sunfire's surface has added warmth to Ruby's skin and has evened out the shadows. The result is more than satisfactory but I'm not happy with the pose so I want to try something else.

Final image

I ask Ruby to lie down on her front and I do the same. As she's very close to the sunfire reflector, the effect is too strong so I turn it over to the white surface. Its effect is far softer and more neutral and, along with the pose, gives a better result.

Shooting in overcast conditions

Cloudy days are a blessing in disguise for portrait photographers. We show you how simple it is to manipulate Mother Nature's softbox for great images

ANYONE WHO LIVES IN THE UK will know we're blessed with more cloudy days than clear skies and sunshine, even in the summer months. For most, this might not sound ideal, but for a portrait photographer it's perfect; a blanket of grey cloud acts as a natural diffuser, providing even, malleable light for you to control with ease using lighting aids such as reflectors. A cloudy day offers the greatest scope for manipulating sunlight as the angle, strength and tone of the light hitting your subject simply depends on what type of reflector you choose to use and how it's positioned. As there's no direct sunlight to contend with, you're also free to place your subject anywhere you please, even at high noon, without having to worry about harsh sunlight creating unsightly shadows and stark highlights. As you're dealing with flat lighting, to add a summer feel to your shots, try to have your subject dress in brightly coloured clothing and find an environment with colour impact, like a lush green field or head to a garden filled with summer flowers.

How well your subject is lit doesn't always depend on your environment, but often your skill using lighting aids. As the light will be descending through the clouds, it is a good idea to position the reflector below and angled upwards towards the subject to fill in any shadows. Also try varying the distance of the reflector from the subject to get the light intensity you're after. If you're dealing with young children, why not have them sit on the reflector: it will fill in any shadows by bouncing the maximum amount of light back onto the subject from the sky and it doubles up as a 'magic carpet' – ideal for keeping those little ones occupied long enough to rattle off a couple of frames. Looking around your environment for reflective surfaces, such as marble or white-coloured walls, can also be useful for bouncing light onto your subject: watch out for colour surfaces though as they will reflect coloured light.

There are several types of reflectors to choose from, with a 5-in-1 kit being the best option for beginners, as they include a gold, white and silver side that vary in reflectance. In some scenarios, though, you may find the silver reflector is too harsh and cool while the gold is too warm. In cases like this, you may want to invest in a mixed reflector such as Lastolite's TriGrip sunfire/slver reflector, which Brett Harkness uses here in the following step-by-step.

Create backlight with flash

More often than not, bright sunshine won't make an appearance when you want it to. So, the next best thing is a flash. Mixing daylight with flash can, from a practical point of view, help fill in any shadows and, from a creative point of view, catapult your images to a new level of dynamism. It's a more advanced technique to tackle, but if you continue to practice it you'll find it opens up a whole range of possibilities. One technique you could try is placing a flashgun behind your subject to mimic a sunlit backlight. As your flash is off-camera, you'll need to be able to trigger it wirelessly. If you're trying this technique for the first time, set your camera to program mode and your flash to TTL. If you find that the flash effect is too low, boost its power by dialling in (positive) flash compensation.

Handling overcast light

Working with kids is tough at the best of times, so shooting in overcast conditions is ideal because you can allow them to move around freely knowing you don't have to worry about harsh shadows or squinting in direct sunshine. We helped Brett Harkness on a typical lifestyle shoot as he worked his magic in very overcast lighting conditions.

Brett's model is a typical eight year-old, unable to sit still for more than a few frames before running off to explore and play. The beauty of a cloudy sky means Brett can let him do this and then when the opportunity arises for a good shot, simply manoeuvre a reflector to improve the quality of light. When photographing your kids, or someone else's, remember to have fun: you're more likely to get better shots of them if you succumb to a few games than if you force them to comply with your shoot.

1 Having scouted the location for suitable backgrounds, Brett started by sitting his subject in front of a green door and set an aperture of f/5.6. As the light levels were low, we positioned a Lastolite sunfire/silver reflector to the side of him to create a little contrast from the flat, low light.

2 With his face in focus, Brett rattled off a few frames, encouraging the subject to give a few different expressions and to mess around with the grass. To get a more dynamic picture, Brett twists his camera to get a diagonal composition.

3 After letting the subject play for a while, Brett sat him on top of a mesh cage to stop him moving around. We held two Lastolite TriGrip reflectors below, and to the side of him, to bounce the light descending from the sky. We used one close to him and the other further away to create slight contrast in his face.

Final image
Brett's series of images captured a variety of expressions and poses. The reflectors worked a treat with the lighting and we used Levels to boost the saturation slightly to give us this final result.

How to take portraits under cover

If you're ever struggling to work with harsh direct sunlight, one easy way
to control the light is to step into some shade. Find out how we go about it...

WHEN THE SUN IS STRONG and high in the sky, there's often nowhere to escape its harsh rays and high-contrast conditions. So if you're after a wide, smooth tonal range with limited contrast and better control and you don't have a diffuser, your best chance for success is to find cover in a spot of shade, such as under a tree or beside a building. Either way placing your subject in some shade instantly improves lighting and gives you more control over the strength and direction of the ambient light. Just remember that the light will be softer, cooler and more diffused, so you'll also have lower light levels to consider, as well as potential and colour casts.

As shade is naturally cooler than sunlight, as well as setting your White Balance to Shade, you may want to opt for a reflector that adds warmth, such as a gold reflector or Lastolite's sunfire/silver reflector. You will also need to be aware of surrounding colours, because dark surfaces absorb light while pale ones reflect it. Watch out for strong coloured surfaces too as they may reflect coloured light, so don't place your subject too close and be aware that you may need to adjust your White Balance settings appropriately, or shoot in Raw so you can correct any colour cast later.

When shooting in shade, you need to be aware of where the light is coming from, which can be tricky as it's likely to be bouncing off different surfaces like walls and floors at various angles, but with practice you'll learn how to master it. By placing your subject in the shade, an easiest way to control the strength and direction of light is to vary the subject's distance from the shade and sun; the closer they are to leaving the shaded area, the stronger the light. You can further control light by moving a reflector towards or away from the subject. You can also control the contrast by where you position your subject, for instance half in the light and half in the shadow or with their back to the light so they're backlit. If you try the latter technique, position a reflector in front of your subject to reflect light onto the face to fill in any shadows. You could also try turning your back to the sun, and have your model face you – it will cast a very flattering, soft and low-contrast light over their face.

Learning how to work with shade is useful when shooting on sunny days, especially if you're dealing with subjects who are wearing clothes that are near white or black in tone, or are dark-skinned, as in bright conditions it can be an exposure nightmare.

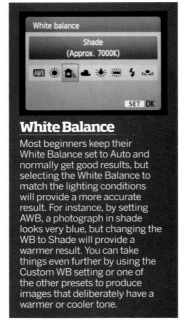

White Balance

Most beginners keep their White Balance set to Auto and normally get good results, but selecting the White Balance to match the lighting conditions will provide a more accurate result. For instance, by setting AWB, a photograph in shade looks very blue, but changing the WB to Shade will provide a warmer result. You can take things even further by using the Custom WB setting or one of the other presets to produce images that deliberately have a warmer or cooler tone.

Shooting in shade

We asked pro photographer Brett Harkness to show us his process for shooting in shade. This alleyway was perfect; it offered some shade and the contained light meant it was soft and easily controllable. To get the right level of light on Emma, his model, he had her walk very slowly from inside the alley, towards him and the light until he was happy with how her face was illuminated.

1 As light levels were low, Brett started with a wide aperture of f/4 and cranked up his ISO to 640 to generate a fast enough shutter speed to shoot handheld. The first few shots he took were good but even though the background is blurred, there's still a lot going on. Brett zoomed his lens in closer to make a tighter head-and-shoulder crop. Much better!

2 For a different shot, he positioned Emma leaning against a wall but by moving her the light on her face was reduced, so he brought in a reflector. We opted for the silver-strong side of the Lastolite Sunfire reflector as it gave the strongest reflectance and filled in a lot of the shadows.

If you're using a wide aperture like f/4 you need to be extremely careful where you place your focus point. Here, Brett has focused on Emma's eyes using selective focusing, which has thrown the foreground and background out of focus. The wall also provides useful lead-in lines to Emma's face, strengthening the composition.

Final image
We picked our favourite and converted it to black & white. Note how the shaded light produces beautifully smooth skin tones.

Shooting late in the day

Daniel Lezano reveals the challenges and rewards of shooting in the final minutes of the day's light

THE 'MAGIC HOUR' IS A PHRASE that's commonly used by landscape photographers to describe the period of time early in the morning or late in the day, when the sun is so low in the sky that the light it casts has a strong golden hue. For landscape images, this type of light can give scenes a three-dimensional feel as the low light creates shadows that reveal the depth and contours of the scenery. For portrait photography, this time of day provides a golden light that will add warmth to a subject's skin tone and backdrop.

Picking this time of day for your shoot has its benefits but also means you have to work fast, because you literally have minutes to take advantage of the setting sun before it disappears. You also need to be aware that you're at the mercy of the weather, as if it's cloudy, you will have little or no golden light to play with. However, if you are lucky enough to have this wonderful light appear, as well as shooting with the subject facing the light, it's also worth using the sunset as a colourful backdrop.

What is also ideal about this time of day is you're guaranteed soft light once the sun has dropped low in the sky, as the entire scene will be in shade. This means that you can work without any lighting aids if you want, although even with low-light levels, you'll find reflectors still produce some illumination, seemingly out of nothing! The extra reflectance will come in useful when trying to avoid camera shake, as the very low light results in a longer shutter speed.

To provide an example of the sort of daylight portrait you could shoot in these conditions, I headed to a local park to capture a couple of shots of a friend's daughter. Ruby has blonde curly hair, which I felt would be good for the late afternoon shoot, backlit by the sunlight. Rather than go for colourful clothing that would contrast with the browns and greens of the park, I arranged for Ruby to wear neutral tones to complement the colour of the scenery more.

With such a short time period to work in, it's best to arrive at your chosen location ten minutes ahead of when you plan to shoot, so you can spot potential viewpoints and backgrounds. I decided to shoot close to the bank of a pond, as it meant the horizon was unobstructed and I would have the light for longer than if I was to shoot within the park where trees would block the falling sun.

I took with me a white, silver and gold reflector, which Ruby's mum was happy to hold in position when required. The white reflector, while a number one choice in most daylight shoots, might prove to be too inefficient to bounce enough daylight when light levels fell very low. In this instance the silver or gold reflector could prove more useful, although care would need to be taken with the gold reflector when combined with the already golden light from the low sun, that it didn't create too warm a cast.

As with the majority of my portrait shoots, I used my DSLR (with 50mm f/1.8 lens) set to aperture-priority, with the initial aperture setting at f/5.6. The White Balance was set to AWB, due to the changing lighting conditions, and I shot in Raw + JPEG, to allow me to tweak WB if necessary in post-production.

Avoiding camera shake

Due to the relatively slow shutter speeds that occur when shooting at this time of day, avoiding camera shake should be at the forefront of your mind. The easiest way to do this is use image stabilisation if your camera or lens has it, stick to a wide aperture of around f/4-5.6 and set the ISO rating to at least 400. You should also use a moderate telephoto lens of between 50mm to 100mm, rather than a longer telephoto, which increase the risk of shake. Using the reciprocal rule can help you determine when you run the risk of shake. To do this, ensure your shutter speed is at least equal or faster than the reciprocal of the lens in use. For instance, if you are using a focal length of 100mm, ensure the shutter speed is at least 1/100sec, at 200mm use 1/200sec or faster, and so on.

1/30sec

1/60sec

With the sun's orb still visible in the sky, I position Ruby in front of a lake, with her back to the sun to make the most of the golden colours of the backdrop. While the low sun creates a glow in her hair, the glare effect is too strong, reducing contrast and adversely affecting the image.

I move Ruby to stand in front of a tree and try shooting from a variety of viewpoints, remembering to alternate the format by taking portrait and landscape images. The texture of the tree adds interest and the golden light from the sun, to Ruby's left, adds a lovely warmth to her skin.

Before the sun has completely set, and the scene becomes totally shaded, the light still has a very slight touch of gold to it, adding colour to her hair. Positioning a white reflector to Ruby's left side allows me to bounce a little extra light in to fill any shadows, yet retain the skin's natural tones.

Going too gold!

Take care with the gold reflector: using it with a setting sun can overdo the warm effect, especially if the reflector is positioned too close to the subject. Save the gold for when the subject is in deep shade and try a silver or white reflector instead.

Gold   White

Final image of the day
By moving further away from Ruby,
I can use some of the scenery to add
visual interest to the image. By shooting
in an upright format and placing Ruby
off-centre, I used the line of trees to lead
the eye through the scene towards her.

FEW OF US HAVE THE LUXURY of a photography studio to hand and the UK's volatile weather means shooting outdoors is not always an option. But don't feel defeated; you can still take stunning portraits indoors regardless of what may seem a daunting plethora of problems to tackle, such as low light, mixed light, limited space and cluttered backgrounds. But we promise you, by the end of this guide, you'll recognise more lighting possibilities, know how to make the most of almost any indoor-lighting scenario and be bursting to try out some of our fun shoots for every room in your house.

One big advantage to shooting portraits at home is that few people feel more relaxed than when surrounded by familiar home comforts, so you may find getting natural-looking expressions and poses easier and quicker. This type of photography is also very inexpensive; there's no need to pay for a studio or props, as a home has everything you need, and your basic set-up need only comprise of a DSLR, a portrait lens (a 50mm is ideal), tripod and possibly a flashgun. Of course, you can introduce accessories too, such as a reflector or softboxes for your flashguns, but you can always centre your shoot around natural light.

Whether you're shooting in your own home or someone else's, it's a good idea to meander around the house in search of natural light sources and scout out locations. Look for windows and interesting décor, as well as neutral backdrops, white walls and low ceilings to bounce flash off if needed. You may get lucky and have a house with a beautiful glass-roofed conservatory, but you may also find yourself scrounging for glimmers of light in dark, cramped rooms, and if this is the case, look to move the shoot to a garage or even the garden shed!

The number one rule for indoor portraits is that there are no rules: the environment dictates the shoot and you have to work with what light you can find or create. For instance, if a room is dark in colour, you may need to bring in studio lighting or a flashgun, or decide to work with it for a low-key or low-light portrait. Alternatively, a light-coloured room can act as a giant softbox, bouncing light off the walls, which is ideal for most shoots and great for high-key images. Available household lighting can offer options too, but be aware of your White Balance as you'll be working with mixed light of different temperatures. The time of day and year also offers benefits and challenges. During winter, most natural light will be gone by 3pm but this just means you can turn your hand to low-light portraits instead. In the summer, however, there is more natural light available, although it will be much stronger too, so it's best to avoid windows in direct sunlight unless you have some heavy diffusion materials handy. The possibilities are endless!

Setting up your digital SLR for indoor portraits

1) EXPOSURE Aperture-priority mode is a good place to start when shooting indoor portraits using available light. By using this semi-automatic mode, you will be able to make the most of limited light by using a wide aperture and shallow depth-of-field to blur distracting backgrounds. If you switch to studioflash, remember to turn your camera to manual mode and dial in the exposure settings having metered the scene.

2) METERING The multi-zone pattern should be more than sufficient for an accurate exposure, but to make sure your shots are sharp when limited lighting is a concern, try raising the ISO rating a couple of stops to increase the shutter speed and avoid shake. Also engage image stabilisation and consider using a tripod, although this will limit your mobility a little. It's better to have a sharp image with some noise than one ruined by blur!

3) FOCUSING While for the most part autofocus will do the job well, it's best to set your camera to central-point focus or to use selective focusing, rather than multi-point AF, as it's likely to pinpoint the nose or eyebrows and not the eyes. Point the central AF point over the eye and half-depress the shutter button to lock focus and then recompose your shot. In very low-light scenarios, you may find that it's easier to switch to manual focus as AF can sometimes struggle in low-contrast situations.

4) WHITE BALANCE While shooting in Raw means you can tweak the White Balance in Photoshop, it's always best to try and get it right in-camera. Working indoors means you may have to tackle mixed lighting and unflattering colour casts. To correct this, take a spot meter reading off a grey card (or white sheet of paper) held in front of your subject's face and use this to set your custom White Balance setting. It will help too if you remember to turn off any indoor lights that are not needed to illuminate the scene, this includes blocking any unneeded windowlight as this can also vary in temperature depending on the time of day.

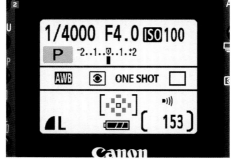

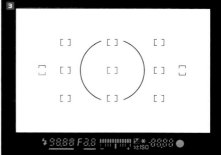

Accessories for indoor portraits

Lenses
As light levels can be limited, ideally use a portrait lens with a wide maximum aperture, such as f/1.8, so you can make the most of the light and create a shallow depth-of-field to blur distracting backgrounds. A 50mm prime lens or the short end of 55-200mm telezoom are good options. A standard zoom like a 18-55mm kit lens is also usable; the widest focal length is ideal for group shots but any wider and at close range in cramped spaces you risk distorting perspective.

Reflectors
When there isn't enough light or it's just too harsh, reflectors are invaluable for filling in shadows. The 5-in-1 version is a great tool, with a white side to reflect clean, neutral light; a silver side for a cool, strong light and a gold for a warm golden glow. There is also a black side to absorb light and a diffuser to soften harsh rays. A Lastolite Triflector is also a very efficient accessory and with three adjustable sides to control the amount and direction of light, it may be all you need.

Flashgun
Your DSLR's built-in flash is suitable for some techniques, but for the most flattering light and more creative options, it's best to invest in a hotshoe-mounted flashgun, which can be triggered off-camera and held at a 45° angle to your model. A flashgun can also be used with accessories like softboxes to make the most of your light without having to invest in an expensive studio set-up.

Flash meter
When you want to bring some studioflash into the set-up, a flash meter is essential. Attach the sync lead and hold the meter in front of the subject's face and press the button to find out the aperture you need to input to achieve a correct exposure.

Flashgun diffusion
A burst of flash from an off-camera light source could save many indoor portraits from being underexposed, but often the glare is too strong for softly-lit, flattering portraits, which is where diffusion accessories come in. The Lastolite Ezybox is brilliant for portraits shot at home, because it's portable and much easier to prepare and put away than a conventional softbox. It comes in two sizes, with the larger version better for photographing groups. Also check out the Strobies Portrait Kit (www.interfitphotographic.com) for more lighting options. You'll also find a number of flash accessories in the gear section of this guide.

Dress to impress

Clothing can really add or detract from a shot, so don't leave it as afterthought. While you need to judge the right clothes based on the style of the shoot, generally in the autumn or winter opt for block colours, whites and creams to brighten up an image, and darker tones for summer portraits. You may also be surprised at how a checked or stripped top can add to an otherwise simple shot. While there's a time and a place for a man's suit, you may find the best shots come from him taking off his tie and his shoes and undoing his top button for a more relaxed look.

Using available light sources

When natural light is in short supply, household lighting may be your only lifeline. We tell you how to make the most of any available light

WHEN YOU'RE SHOOTING INDOORS, you need to make the most of any available light. During the day, this may be in the form of sunlight streaming through a window or patio doors, or the soft diffused light flooding in through a netted window.

Covering all the various options to controlling and manipulating daylight indoors could fill a tome, but there are a few basic lighting principles that if applied properly, pretty much guarantee great results.

The light indoors will usually be diffused and non-directional as it has bounced off walls, the ceiling and floor, which means it's already flattering for portraits. Should you have strong light streaming in, use net curtains, or hang a sheet of muslin or other thin, white, diffusing material over the window to soften the light. Alternatively, move the subject away from the window to soften the light falling on them.

Regardless of the nature of the light or its intensity, the one accessory you should have to hand is a reflector. This lighting aid will help you get the most out of even the smallest amount of light by bouncing ambient light back on to a subject's face. If you haven't got one already, invest in a silver/white reflector or better still, a 3-in-1 reflector that also includes a gold surface.

If you're struggling for a neutral background, stand your model in front of a window for an instant white backdrop and bounce sunlight back onto the face with a reflector. Alternatively,

stand with your back to the window and have the model look out to get an even soft light over their face or, if you want more shadow, stand them side on to a window and fill in with a reflector on the other side. Usually the bigger the window the softer the light and, with a big window behind you, it can also be used to give the model's eyes an interesting catchlight.

At night, available light is pretty much limited to room lighting, in particular the traditional tungsten bulb, halogen lights built into ceiling panels, spotlights and, in the majority of kitchens, fluorescent lighting. All have very different characteristics in terms of how they distribute light, from focused beams of a spotlight, to the non-directional spread of a tungsten bulb, which should be explored to find the best way they can be used to light the subject effectively. Also, remember that each has its own colour temperature, so be sure to set the appropriate White Balance preset to get accurate colours, or use a test shot of a grey card to set a custom WB setting on your DSLR (your camera's instructions will explain how).

Another option to try is to use an 'incorrect' White Balance setting to produce images that exhibit a strong cool or warm cast that adds mood to the scene. Whichever method you decide to use, we'd strongly recommend you shoot in Raw as you can then easily tweak White Balance when converting images from Raw to JPEG on your computer.

The bathtub 'reflector'!

Unless you have an avocado or pink suite, a bathroom could be the only room in the house where you have access to clean, white light. It can be a great place to maximise natural light as the white surfaces of the walls replicate a similar effect to a giant softbox. If the light is still limited, however, you could try placing your subject in a white bathtub as light will bounce off the sides to mimic the job of a reflector – this technique is ideal for 'little people'. You could also bounce flash off the sides of the tub for a similar effect.

BRETT HARKNESS

BRETT HARKNESS

BRETT HARKNESS

Above: Add mood and mystery

Windowlight is perfect for flattering portraits. Try adding an air of mystery to your image by having the subject look contemplative out the window and avoid eye contact. Underexpose the image slightly to darken the subject a little.

Left: Doing it for the kids!

Be prepared for anything when photographing children. Be ready as soon as you step through the front door, so you don't miss any opportunities to take a candid picture.

Back to a window

For an even light across your model's face, stand with your back to a window and shoot your model facing towards the windowlight.

Shoot a windowlit portrait!

STEWART BYWATER:
When the unpredictable British weather prevents you from heading outside, one really easy technique to try indoors is to take a windowlit portrait. Many master portrait photographers have said that they actually prefer windowlight to any artificial light source, as it provides more natural results and can be controlled in a number of ways, such as by diffusing it with net curtains, various kinds of paper, or using a reflector to bounce light back onto your subject. This is one of the most traditional and simple photographic techniques around, and will give you great results, whatever the weather! My subject for the session was Bob, a neighbour of mine, who kindly agreed to sit for me. Bob looks much younger than his age (he's 80), but he has a great deal of character in his face – this is something to consider when choosing your subject, especially if you want to convert it to black & white.

Get ready!

⏱ **TIME REQUIRED**
20 MINUTES

📷 **EQUIPMENT NEEDED**
NIKON D700 WITH 105MM MACRO LENS & TRIPOD

➕ **ALSO USED**
5-IN-1 REFLECTOR

Get a helping hand!
If you're without an assistant, ask your subject to hold the reflector off to the side.

Using a reflector

When shooting a windowlit portrait, such as this, with your subject side-on to the window, one side of the face will be brightly lit, while the other will remain in shadow. This can create a very striking, high-contrast look, but that's not always the look that you'll be after. A simple way to compensate for the uneven lighting is to use a reflector, to bounce light back onto the parts of your subject's face that are in shadow. Here, I have used the *Digital SLR Photography*'s 5-in-1 reflector, and below you can see the effect that each of the different coloured sides makes to Bob's face.

None

White

Silver

Gold

1 First of all, I placed a stool by the window. It's important to choose the right place, taking into account where the subject's face will be. The trick is to ensure the light falls directly onto the face. I then set up my tripod and mounted the camera on it. I looked through the viewfinder to make sure that the camera was the right distance from Bob for the close-up shot I wanted.

2 Once everything was in place, I asked Bob to position himself in a comfortable pose. I set the camera to ISO 200 (the lowest native setting on the D700), with an aperture of f/2.8, as I just wanted to keep Bob's eyes and the front of his face in focus, throwing the background into a blur. I then took a few quick shots, and reviewed them on the camera's LCD screen.

3 Because of the low light, I was getting longer shutter speeds than I wanted, which made any slight movement on Bob's part really show up. Some of his facial features were also slightly blurred, due to the shallow depth-of-field, so I increased the ISO to 1000, and stopped the aperture down to f/5.6, giving me a slightly faster shutter speed and an increased depth-of-field.

4 I took a few pictures of Bob looking straight at the camera, but the images didn't capture his vivacious character; so I engaged him in conversation. Bob looks remarkably young for his 80 years, and has a great sense of humour, so by provoking a bit of emotion in his face, it showed up more of his laughter lines and added a bit more interest to the shots.

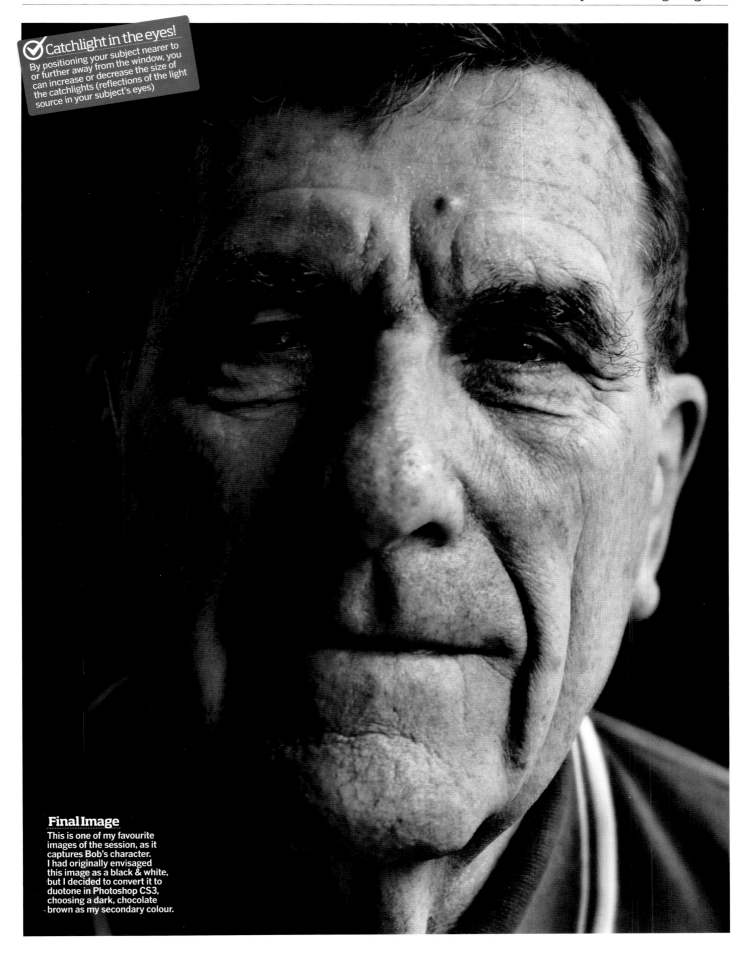

✓ Catchlight in the eyes!
By positioning your subject nearer to or further away from the window, you can increase or decrease the size of the catchlights (reflections of the light source in your subject's eyes)

Final Image
This is one of my favourite images of the session, as it captures Bob's character. I had originally envisaged this image as a black & white, but I decided to convert it to duotone in Photoshop CS3, choosing a dark, chocolate brown as my secondary colour.

Shoot a simple contemporary portrait

DANIEL LEZANO: Many leading lifestyle portrait photographers use nothing more than ambient daylight for the vast majority of their portrait shoots. So, when we have the benefits of bright, sunny days at our disposal, we should use it to capture some simple yet effective portraits of family and friends. The best thing about shooting lifestyle portraits is that you can do it with the minimum amount of equipment – your DSLR with a kit lens is enough – although I'm using my favourite optic, the humble (and cheap!) 50mm f/1.8 lens. Due to the unpredictable nature of daylight, lighting aids such as a reflector and a diffuser can come in handy too, but aren't essential. The key thing to remember is that you want to capture a 'clean' image, in other words try to keep the subject and the setting as simple as possible. I've opted for the classic combination of having my subject, Bethany, wear a white top and jeans, and shot her lying on my dining room's laminate flooring.

Get ready!

TIME REQUIRED
15 MINUTES

EQUIPMENT NEEDED
CANON EOS 5D MKII
WITH 50MM F/1.8

EQUIPMENT NEEDED
SILVER REFLECTOR
AND LASTOLITE
DIFFUSER

Shoot at a slant

One compositional trick that most lifestyle photographers apply to their images is to slant the camera so that the images are captured with an uneven horizon. This simple technique adds a little energy into the image and is very effective – just take care not to tilt the camera too far.

Take care with focus!
You need to ensure your focusing is precise as using a wide aperture, which gives limited depth-of-field, leaves little margin for error. Select single-point AF, lock the focus on the eye and recompose

ABOVE: My dining room is quite small, so I've had to clear it completely of furniture. As my subject will be lying on the floor, I vacuum it to ensure it's as clean as possible. Due to the cramped space, I open the patio doors in case I need to shoot from the patio. However, I'll start by shooting from within the room and use the white walls as a neutral backdrop. Using a wide aperture to give a shallow depth-of-field is ideal for this type of shot and I'll be trying out my 50mm's maximum aperture of f/1.8, although I'll take most of the images at f/2.5-3.5 as it will improve sharpness.

Diffused daylight

For flattering portraits, the light should be as diffused as possible to avoid your model squinting in direct sunlight or having the light on their face too harsh. In this instance, try to reposition them so they're in the shade or use a diffuser to shade the scene (inset right). If neither of these work, you may need to wait until the sun's position changes or shoot when the sky is more overcast. A silver reflector is handy even when shooting in non-directional light to fill in shadows.

1 My first shot is just a tester for composition and exposure. I've a pretty clear idea in my head of the type of shot I'm looking for, with Bethany lying down with her lower legs and feet bent back towards her head. This shot isn't bad, but the side-lighting causes her right side to be too dark.

2 I place a silver reflector to Bethany's right just out of frame and it makes a noticeable difference, bouncing back enough light to even out the lighting on the face. The lighting's better, but the wall behind, while plain, causes the whole scene to appear a little too cramped for my liking.

Final image
My next shot is perfect and all I need to do is apply minimal post-production. I've boosted the contrast in Curves and cropped the image slightly to give me the result I set out to shoot. Give it a try – you'll be surprised just how easy it is to shoot a great lifestyle portrait at home.

3 I shift Bethany and my position so that I'm now shooting into the room from the patio rather than from the side. I close the blinds in the backdrop to darken the background. The empty space created behind her is an improvement over the original set-up but my viewpoint is too high.

4 I crouch down and the lower viewpoint is far better. However, the multi-zone meter has bleached out Bethany's face due to the dark background causing it to overexpose the scene. This is easily taken care of by dialling in some negative exposure compensation. I find -2/3EV is ideal.

Project: Rooms with a view

Paul Ward shows us the huge potential for shooting portraits in every room in the house

WE CHALLENGED pro-portrait photographer Paul Ward to capture a great portrait in every room of a house within one hour, using different light sources and techniques that showed off what's possible with available light, flash and imagination. As you'll discover, despite the time constraints, Paul managed to creatively use windowlight, flash, candles and even Christmas lights, as well as the humble household light bulb! By the end, you'll have no doubt as to the potential your home offers for you to shoot great indoor portraits. Make sure you give it a go soon!

1) Master bedroom: Diffused windowlight

On entry to the bedroom, Paul instantly earmarked the window and mirror as an ambient light source and interesting backdrop, so he positioned Rebecca side-on to the net-curtained window and tried a couple of ideas. Firstly, he asked Rebecca to turn her head away from the window so as to use the light from the window as a white backdrop. By doing this her face fell into shade, so a friend held a reflector to the side of Rebecca to bounce window light back onto her face. Next, he asked her to look towards the window and to create some extra shadow, held the curtain open slightly. As there was limited room for a tripod, Paul set his DSLR to manual mode and set the lens to its widest aperture of f/2.8, which gave a shutter speed of 1/60sec at ISO 800.

3) Lounge: One tungsten light bulb

A single light bulb can be efficient in creating shots high in contrast, as it's a sharp light source that will produce harsh shadows. Try and get the light bulb head-height with the model and position it in front of the model's face and the camera to minimise shadows. Either set your camera to a high ISO with an aperture of f/2.8 or wider, or put the camera on a tripod and get your model to stand very still. Remember to switch the White Balance to Tungsten too!

2) Dining room: Candlelight

Make sure the room is dark and light some candles on a table. You will need your sitter to get as close as possible to the light for their face to be illuminated and, to avoid a high ISO, ask them to remain very still. Set an aperture of at least f/2.8 in aperture-priority mode to maximise light. If you struggle using autofocus, switch to manual or LiveView and tweak the focusing.

4) Loft: Bounce flash

The principle for this shot can be applied to any room that has white walls or a white ceiling. Paul used this statement wallpaper as a background but, as the rest of the room is white, he was able to bounce one flash off a wall behind him to illuminate Rebecca evenly. Although this can be enough, Paul also fired a second flash into a Brolly to illuminate her at a 45° angle.

5) Guest bedroom: Christmas lights

This shot can be done in any room that's completely dark. Drape Christmas lights across, or wrap them around, your subject's body. You will need to use a high ISO of at least 800 and a wide aperture, such as f/1.8, so a 50mm lens is ideal. As long as you place some lights on or near the face, your camera's autofocus should lock on to the subject but, if not, switch to manual focus.

6) Bathroom: Diffused windowlight

Shutters are useful for controlling harsh sunlight and in this bathroom set-up they were necessary as the light increased in strength as the shoot progressed. Having taken a test shot in manual mode, I knew f/6.3 was too narrow an aperture as even at ISO 800 it underexposed the scene. I opened the aperture to f/4 and stopped down from 1/160sec to 1/125sec and ISO 400 to reduce noise. I asked Rebecca to angle herself side-on to the window as space was limited, and this also provided some contrast with the aid of the blinds across her face. While normally altering the White Balance setting to match the lighting (in this case Daylight) turns in the best results, I also tried a Tungsten WB to give a creative blue cast.

Tungsten WB

Add a warm feel to winter images

Find out how to photograph a low-light portrait in front of a log fire

There's nothing quite like curling up in front of a roaring log fire when it's freezing cold outside. The fire light elicits a feeling of warmth and comfort, which can also make atmospheric portrait lighting. Unfortunately a fire doesn't throw out as much light as you might think, so you will often have to rely on slow shutter speeds and high ISO ratings. You could use a tripod to reduce the risk of camera shake, but you'll still need to be careful that your subject stays still so not to ruin the shot.

Using a lens with a fast maximum aperture, such as a 50mm f/1.8, helps when shooting in limited light and has the bonus of providing an attractively shallow depth-of-field. Even working with an aperture of f/1.8, you may need to set your ISO to 800 or even 1250 to get a fast enough shutter speed to combat motion blur. Don't go any slower than 1/60sec, otherwise your subject may appear unsharp. Although you'll be working with low light levels, you can expect quite a lot of contrast in the shot, so using autofocus should not be a problem. But if

you do find the camera struggles to lock focus on the eyes, switch to using manual focus. Bear in mind that when working with a wide aperture like f/1.8, and shallow depth-of-field, you have to be extremely careful to focus in the right place so the image is not rendered out of focus.

There is a fair amount of experimentation involved with this kind of shot, so make sure you have a very cooperative subject and be aware of how hot they can get close to the fire. A log fire is often a point of interest for people so it doesn't look unnatural to have someone gazing into it. If a child can be mesmerised by the flames long enough to sit still you could capture some great child portraits, or try positioning a couple in front of the fire with a bottle of wine for a romantic portrait instead. Cats and dogs often lie in front of a log fire and can be perfect subjects for this type of shot. Professional photographer Paul Ward shows us how he created this beautiful atmospheric shot of Megan in her family home using a budget lens: the Canon EOS 50mm f/1.8.

Take steamy portraits outside

An effective way to evoke a sense of warmth in an outdoor winter portrait is to capture a subject bundled in winter clothing clasping a steaming drink. As it's the steam rising from the liquid that gives the photograph atmosphere, you need to find a way to enhance it while also lighting your subject well. While you may be able to see the steam clearly, the camera can struggle to pick it up. To help with this, position your subject so the steam is in front of a dark background with the sun behind to help illuminate the steam – with a light background the steam won't show up.

Light background   Dark background

ISO640

ISO1250

1 I first did a couple of test shots in aperture-priority mode, with the camera set to f/1.8 to let in the maximum amount of light. I found that to shoot handheld I had to increase the ISO from 640 to 1250 to expose Megan and get a fast enough shutter speed to reduce the risk of motion blur.

2 In aperture-priority, the camera reacts to the changing light on Megan's face, sometimes overexposing it, and I tended to get different results for each shot. So once I had an idea of the best exposure (1/60sec to 1/100sec at f/1.8, ISO 1250), I selected manual mode to get the same results every time.

3 Next I tried to see if repositioning Megan on the other side of the fire improved the light on her face. Unfortunately, the natural parting of her hair meant it covered her face, creating shadows. Returning her to the original side, I also asked her to tie her hair back to see if it improved the shots.

4 To enhance the glow, I experimented with the White Balance setting to see if I could make it slightly warmer. Once I got the image I liked, I tried converting the image to black & white in Photoshop (Layer>New Adjustment Layer>Black & White), but it killed the atmosphere completely.

Final image

This was my favourite image of the shoot. Asking Megan to pull her hair back has allowed the fire light to illuminate her face with minimal shadows. You could get a similar result shooting a portrait by candlelight, if you don't have a log fire.

Basics for creative flash

Using flash creatively requires an understanding of the relationship between ambient light and flash

USING FLASH ISN'T AS DIFFICULT as it once was, but it is a little more involved than shooting with only ambient light. When you take a picture in daylight, the light source (the sun) is constant and you can see how it falls on your subject. You can't do this with flash as it only bursts on to the scene once you've pressed the shutter and, to see its effects, you need to review the image on the LCD monitor. Judging exposure is easier with ambient light too – with experience you can tell if a subject may be over- or underexposed based on the lighting conditions. With flash, to get the lighting just as you want it, there is a little more trial and error involved. Thankfully, using flash is far easier than ever before.

In fact, getting a correct exposure using flash is extremely easy as the camera's TTL (Through The Lens) metering takes care of this for you. The trick with flash is not so much getting the right exposure, but setting it up to get the creative effect you want. In other words, how you'd like the flash to illuminate your subject, how you'd like to balance the flash exposure with the ambient light, and whether you want to use more than one flash unit to achieve more advanced creative results.

Using flash creatively is all about experimenting with exposures to get the best possible results by tapping into the versatility of your flash. If you take a photo with your flash set in auto, you'll normally find that the subject appears well exposed but the background is very dark or black. Do you know why this is and do you know how to take the same shot again and avoid this problem? Learning to set an exposure that allows more ambient light to be recorded in the scene, to balance with the flash, is a very simple example of understanding how creative flash can benefit your photography and help you take better pictures. We provide the answer to this question as well as easy-to-follow advice that will help you take some exciting and creative images with your camera's built-in flash and/or an external flashgun. If you don't own a flashgun, we'd recommend you save up for one or add it to your gift list for a birthday or Christmas. As you'll discover, thanks to the sophistication of digital SLRs and dedicated flashguns, creative flash photography is far easier and much more fun than ever before!

Flash accessories for creative flash

■ **DEDICATED OFF-CAMERA LEADS:** The hotshoe isn't always the best place for your flashgun, especially when you want to get creative! Ask your local photo dealer about the various leads (also known as off-camera cords) available for your camera. As well as branded leads, you'll find dedicated cords from the likes of Hama, Lastolite and Interfit, ranging from 0.6m to ten metres! Prices start from as little as £20.

■ **WIRELESS TTL FLASH CONTROL:** The off-camera cord is a great option but wireless, or remote control flash as it's also termed, is becoming increasingly affordable. Attach a transmitter to your hotshoe and a receiver to the flashgun and you can operate wirelessly at distances up to 100m. Most brands have their own dedicated units but these are expensive. We'd recommend units from independents as they're far more affordable. In particular, the £60 Hahnel Combi TF (www.hahnel.ie) is brilliant value for money.

■ **FLASH GELS:** These inexpensive sheets of colour gels are attached by Velcro or bands to the front of your flash head to change the colour of its flash output. We'd recommend kits from Lumiquest (www.newprouk.co.uk) and Honl (www.flaghead.co.uk), which are made of high quality materials yet are very affordable.

Wireless flash on a budget

■ **SLAVE CELLS:** All you need to try out wireless flash is a cheap and cheerful slave cell, such as Hama's £12 slave unit. Slip this on an off-camera flash and when it detects your on-camera flash's output, it will trigger the remote flash. You won't be able to provide any TTL control for your remote flashgun, but it's an ideal option for when the remote flash is used in manual, such as when using flash gels.

■ **SLAVE FLASH/BUDGET FLASHGUNS:** There are a number of affordable flashguns that lack any form of sophistication but boast an integrated slave cell, which makes them the perfect choice for use as a remote manual flashgun. You could also buy literally any flashgun made for digital/film SLRs that offer manual power settings and slip a slave cell to its base, allowing you to experiment with wireless flash set-ups. We've even used a 1970s Olympus Trip flashgun with success!

Setting flash modes on your DSLR

You can access flash modes via your camera's menu to control flash exposures taken using the integral or external flashgun. The set-up is similar on most models from the same brand.

CANON EOS 500D/550D/600D

(1) Press MENU and scroll down the first tab to the Flash control option.

(2) Press SET to bring up the various Flash control options. By selecting either the Built-in flash or External flash function settings, you're able to choose facilities such as second-curtain sync or flash exposure compensation.

NIKON D60/D3000/D3100

(1) Press and hold the flash button and turn the input dial to change flash modes. To set flash exposure compensation, press and hold the flash and exposure compensation buttons and turn the input dial.

(2) With the D3000 and more recent models, you can also press the i button, then use the four-way control to select and set the various flash options.

OLYMPUS E-400/500-SERIES

(1) Press the flash button to pop up the flash and press again to bring up the flash modes on the LCD monitor.

(2) Rotate the thumb dial to choose a flash mode and press OK to set it.

(3) Press MENU and go to the fourth tab for Custom Functions, which has a couple more flash options.

PENTAX K-SERIES

(1) Press the down button of the four-way control to select flash modes. Use the left/right of the four-way control to select flash modes.

(2) While on the flash mode screen, you can use the input dial to set flash exposure compensation.

SONY ALPHA SERIES

(1) Press the Fn button and select the Flash mode box for access to various options.

(2) Press MENU and go to the first tab for other flash options including flash exposure compensation.

(3) To deactivate the flash, set the mode dial to Flash-off.

External flashguns: Main features

A dedicated flashgun offers far more power than is available on your integral unit and provides a number of very useful facilities too.

1) FLASH HEAD: Direct flash can prove harsh, so most models have heads that can be raised and angled to provide 'bounce flash' (the term used when the light from the flash is bounced off surfaces such as walls and ceiling to provide a softer, more flattering effect). The heads in many flashguns have a zoom facility, which allows the flash coverage to better match the focal length of the lens being used. Better specified models have a flip-up diffuser panel to soften the flash output – useful if your subject is within a couple of metres.

2) AF ASSIST LAMP: In low light, this lamp can send out a beam or a burst of infrared light to aid the camera's AF system.

3) LCD PANEL: While many flashguns have a scale or series of buttons, the more sophisticated models have a large LCD panel with icons to help make selecting modes easier.

4) FUNCTION BUTTONS: More advanced flash units have a selection of buttons and dials, most usually handling more than one function. It can be tricky at first to understand what each one does, so keep the instructions handy and experiment!

Flash modes for creative effect

If you've never really experimented with flash, then you may well have left your camera set to autoflash, which sets a fast shutter speed to avoid shake and ensures the flash correctly exposes the subject. It's a mode that works well for general snapshots, but isn't the mode to choose for creative effects. For that, these are the flash modes you need to master:

SLOW-SYNC: This mode sets a slow shutter speed that allows ambient light in the scene to be recorded, while the flash ensures that the subject is correctly exposed. This mode is set automatically when using a Canon EOS in aperture-priority mode.

REAR: Normally, when you take a flash exposure, the flashgun fires at the start of the exposure. With this mode, the flash fires at the end of the exposure, which is useful when shooting moving subjects as the trail of light streams behind rather than in front of them.

FP/ HIGH SPEED: All cameras have a standard flash sync speed, which is the fastest shutter speed that can be used with flash. The high-speed flash mode, available with some flashguns, allows a camera to use flash at any shutter speed up to its maximum.

WIRELESS: When using an external flashgun, you'll normally slip it on to the camera's hotshoe, or use it off-camera via a dedicated lead. With this function, you can fire the flashgun without the need for any leads or additional accessories. It's worth noting that there are two main forms of wireless flash. The first is the dedicated system, where the flashgun(s) and the transmitter are designed to communicate together to provide accurate exposures. There is often the option to control the balance of the various flashguns via a hotshoe-mounted unit. The other main type is the non-dedicated wireless system, which is a budget method that we use for our flash gels technique. This system relies on using flashguns in manual mode with slave cells.

Flash terms

GUIDE NUMBER (GN): This indicates the flashgun's power: the higher the number, the greater the power. In manual flash mode, if you divide the Guide Number by the camera-to-subject distance in meters you'll get the right aperture for a decent exposure.

FLASH COVERAGE: The spread of light across the frame. It's stated as a lens focal length (e.g. 18mm). Use a lens wider than stated and the light falls off towards the edges of the frame, leading to dark corners.

FLASH EXPOSURE COMPENSATION (FEC): This facility overrides the flash exposure set automatically by the camera, much like you would with ambient light and exposure compensation. Set a positive value to boost flash output and a negative value to reduce it.

THROUGH THE LENS (TTL): The exposure system within the camera communicates with the flash to ensure perfect exposures by evaluating the flash output.

How exposure modes work with flash
Not all brands handle flash the same way, so be sure to use the correct mode!*

BRAND	CANON	NIKON	PENTAX	OLYMPUS	SONY
PROGRAM MODE	Camera sets shutter speed and aperture, but raises shutter speed to avoid camera shake. Background may be dark.	Camera sets exposure, but raises shutter speed to avoid camera shake, unless slow sync mode is set. Background may be dark.	Camera sets exposure, but raises shutter speed to avoid camera shake, unless slow sync mode is set. Background may be dark.	Camera sets exposure, but raises shutter speed to avoid camera shake, unless slow sync mode is set. Background may be dark.	Camera sets exposure, but raises shutter speed to avoid camera shake, unless slow sync mode is set. Background may be dark.
APERTURE-PRIORITY	User picks aperture; camera calculates flash exposure accordingly. Shutter speed is picked to render ambient light correctly. Be aware of camera shake.	User picks the aperture and the camera selects flash exposure accordingly. Shutter speed is limited to prevent camera shake, unless slow-sync mode is selected.	User sets aperture and camera sets shutter speed to correctly expose background, up to the maximum sync speed. Risk of camera shake in low light.	User picks aperture and camera selects flash exposure accordingly. Shutter speed limited to prevent camera shake, unless slow-sync mode is also selected.	User picks aperture and camera selects flash exposure accordingly. Shutter speed limited to prevent camera shake, unless slow-sync mode is also selected.
SHUTTER-PRIORITY	User picks shutter speed and camera picks corresponding aperture for ambient light, then calculates flash output according to this aperture.	User picks shutter speed and camera picks corresponding aperture to expose ambient light correctly, then calculates flash output according to this aperture.	User picks shutter speed and camera picks corresponding aperture to expose ambient light properly, then calculates flash output according to this aperture.	User picks shutter speed and camera picks corresponding aperture to expose ambient light correctly, then calculates flash output according to this aperture.	User picks shutter speed and camera picks corresponding aperture to expose ambient light correctly, then calculates flash output according to this aperture.
EXPOSURE COMPENSATION	Affects ambient light exposure only.	Affects ambient and flash exposure.	Affects ambient and flash exposure.	Affects ambient light exposure only.	Affects ambient and flash exposure.
FLASH EXPOSURE COMPENSATION	Affects flash exposure only.	Affects flash exposure only.	Affects flash exposure only.	Affects flash exposure only.	Affects flash exposure only.

* Please note that the stated information relates to most general shooting conditions. However, in certain situations, the camera and flash will operate differently.

Simulate low evening sunlight

Learn how to use off-camera flash to create attractive hairlight

When using flash to light a portrait, the first thing most photographers do is point it at the subject's face, but by placing it behind the model's head you can create attractive hairlight – adding a different dimension to the image. It's a great, creative technique to try in the winter months too, when you don't fancy going outdoors but want to simulate the look of a low evening sun from the warmth of your home.

To get the best results, the subject should ideally have curly or wavy hair and be placed in front of a dark background to accentuate the light. You'll also need to experiment with your flash's power to find a balance between overpowering the ambient light and getting the right spread through the hair. For instance, if you're doing a full-body portrait, a burst of flash at 1/2 power would work best, while a head shot might require only 1/4 power. It's worth playing with the distance of your flash to your subject's head as well, but make sure the flash is completely hidden so it diffuses through the hair. Also consider your aperture: minimal depth-of-field will soften the spread of light while a narrow aperture will produce a star-like effect from the flash.

Reflectors

You can use your camera's integral flash unit to illuminate the face, or you could use a reflector instead to bounce some olight on to the subject's face. You can control the tone of the light by the choice of your reflector too. If you want a cool tone, opt for a silver reflector, or for a warm cast try a gold reflector. Alternatively, why not try Lastolite's TriGrip Sunfire or Sunlite reflector, like we've used in this step-by-step, as it has strips of silver and gold for a more natural cast. If you only have a silver or gold reflector you could always experiment with your image's White Balance in camera or Adobe Camera Raw to warm it up or cool the tone down.

Backlighting a portrait with flash

Professional lifestyle photographer Brett Harkness frequently uses his off-camera flash behind his subjects, whether to create a dramatic burst of light behind a full-body portrait or to add a subtle, attractive hairlight to a head shot. He shows us how…

Without reflector

With reflector

1 (Above) To start with, we position Emma in a doorway so we can use natural light to fill in the shadows on her face. During the winter months, however, when light levels are low you may need to use a reflector or a second flash to light her face, held approximately three or four feet away so not to overpower the backlight. With the camera and flash set to manual, I dial in f/5.6 and ISO 500, because of the relatively low light, and place the flashgun on the step behind Emma.

2 (Right) I take a test shot of Emma at f/5.6 with the flash behind her set to 1/8 power and no reflector. As you can see, the flash isn't strong enough to have any effect and her face is underexposed. So I set the flash to 1/4 power and ask my assistant to hold a reflector a few feet away from Emma's face to fill in the shadows.

3 (Left) As I can see the stairs in the background of the pictures, I add a blanket over the steps to get rid of the white line and darken the background to enhance the backlight.

4 (Above) You may also want to try playing with your camera's White Balance settings to see what effect it has on the picture. Normally if you're working with flash you would set Flash or Custom WB, but why not try Daylight or Tungsten to alter the tone of the image? Alternatively you could shoot in Raw and play with the WB in post-production.

Final image
With slight tweaks to the contrast in Photoshop and a little skin softening, we're left with a beautiful portrait.

How to add drama to sky for outdoor portraits

Underexposing the scene and using flash to light the subject is a great way to add impact to portraits

More often than not, flash is used to balance flash and ambient lighting or to fill in shadows, but now and again, it pays to use flash to overpower the ambient light and completely transform a scene.

A great technique to try, and one often used by the pros, is to capture a dramatic sky by underexposing the scene, leading it to appear far darker than it does in reality, while allowing the flash to correctly expose the subject. There are two ways that you can do this: by using the exposure compensation facility to dial in a negative value, or by working in manual mode, both of which we'll explain in further detail.

Regardless of which one you choose to use, for the best results, you should avoid using the camera's integral flash or mounting a flash on the hotshoe and instead trigger a remote flash via slave or an off-camera flash cord. By simply repositioning the flash to the side of the subject, you immediately change the function of the flash from a flat fill-in light to one that's directional and contrast-enhancing. For the purpose of this step-by-step, we'll explain how to do this technique using manual settings rather than relying on your camera's TTL system, as it offers a greater control and a chance to learn and experiment.

Different camera and flash systems work in different ways, so if you do want to try the exposure compensation method with TTL, check your camera's instruction manual.

It's important to remember when working with manual flash that the shutter speed controls the amount of ambient light reaching the sensor, while aperture controls flash output. And for this technique, your shutter speed is paramount as you're exposing for the sky, not the subject. The faster the shutter speed, the darker the ambience will be: the slower the shutter speed the more you encourage the influence of ambient light.

Using radio triggers

Most of the time, once a flash is off-camera and triggered by a radio release it loses its TTL capabilities, so it's important your flash has manual settings. To retain TTL, you could opt for a dedicated off-camera lead, but you will be restricted by the length of the cord. However, if you're comfortable using manual flash, the more affordable option is a slave cell (see p60) or a flash remote trigger and there are many available, varying in price and functions. While PocketWizards are brilliant, and a market leader for performance, they're also expensive. Camera manufacturers also have their own remotes but we'd recommend independent versions by the likes of Calumet, Kenro, Hahnel and Seculine as they're cheaper and do the job well enough. The Hahnel Combi TF, for instance, is a bargain at around £60 and doubles up as a remote flash trigger and shutter release. Seculine's highly-efficient Twin Link T2D Wireless Radio Flash Trigger kit can be bought for around £120. Regardless of what remote you buy, remember you need a transmitter to sit on your camera's hotshoe and a receiver to attach to each of your off-camera flashguns for it to work.

Using exposure compensation

Instead of using manual mode, set your camera to aperture-priority mode, your flash to TTL and meter for the background. Dial in the aperture you want and then set a negative value on the camera's exposure compensation to at least two stops to underexpose the scene: the flash will take care of the subject. If you're shooting with a Nikon, you may have to increase your flash exposure compensation by two stops too as the flash and exposure compensation are linked. Have a play and experiment with results.

Getting a dramatic sky with an outdoor portrait

This is an advanced technique, so requires practice. Pro photographer Brett Harkness, who regularly uses it, explains how to make the most of manual flash and moody skies. On this shoot, it's overcast and there's a mass of detail in the sky to capture. As Brett likes his shots sharp front to back, he uses a small aperture of around f/13 and sets his flash to 1/4 power to compensate. If you want shallow depth-of-field, keep the flash close to your subject, set the flash to 1/8 power and open the aperture.

1 (Above) I ask my assistant to hold the flashgun several feet away from the model, Emma, and because we're not using any diffusion accessories, I have him hold the flash vertically to get a bigger spread of light over her body. I add sunglasses and gold fabric for a fashion-shoot feel.

2 (Right) To capture a moody sky, I have to dramatically underexpose the scene using a fast shutter speed to retain the detail in the sky. As you can see from this picture, a fast shutter speed has underexposed the scene but without using flash it means the subject is also very dark.

3 (Left) Once I start using flash, my shutter speed is immediately limited to the camera's sync speed – in this case 1/250sec. With my camera set to manual mode, I set the aperture that gives the scene the correct exposure for the ambient light. I set the flashgun to 1/4 power, which exposes Emma well, but the scene lacks drama and mood.

4 (Below) To improve the effect from the flash, my assistant raises the flash and points it down on Emma. However, the key to darkening the scene behind her is to close down the aperture (in this instance by two stops) so that the background is underexposed, resulting in a far moodier result.

Final image
With a few tweaks to the Curves and Levels in Photoshop, Brett's produced a dramatic portrait with a single off-camera flash. Give it a go!

Add colour with flash gels

Try out our inexpensive and simple wireless flash technique

Getting to use just one flashgun proves a daunting prospect for many, so how does the thought of using two grab you? This technique deals with showing you how to light a subject with one flashgun, while a second flash is used to illuminate the background. This technique is useful when you want to highlight detail in the scene or, as shown here, you want to use flash gels to light it in a completely different colour.

While the technique may sound incredibly difficult, it's actually quite easy to achieve. You need to use your camera's integral flash (or a hotshoe-mounted flashgun) to illuminate your subject, which is pretty straightforward as the exposure is taken care of automatically by the camera thanks to the wonders of TTL flash. A second flashgun is triggered automatically by the main flash to illuminate the background, so you've little to do other than ensure that the remote flash is set up correctly, which as the panel on the right reveals, is pretty easy to do. And, if you think this sounds expensive, our panel on wireless flash on a

budget, which you'll find on page 50, should quickly dispel this myth too!

Flash gels are essentially small sheets of coloured plastic that are placed over the flash head to colour the flash output. The flash gel is held in place over the head via Velcro or an elastic band and with a number of kits available with a choice of colours, it's an inexpensive and easy way to add creative flash effects to your images. Incidentally, larger flash gel kits are available that can be used with studioflash heads too, and in fact, the technique we've used here can easily be applied to studioflash set-ups as well as flashguns.

Using flash gels to illuminate a background is equally suited to both indoor and outdoor locations. Plain backdrops as well as textured surfaces are suitable, although the latter does provide additional visual interest. It's also worth bearing in mind that you can use more than one flashgun for the background, so feel free to mix colour gels. The key is to experiment as much as possible, as this is when creative photos present themselves.

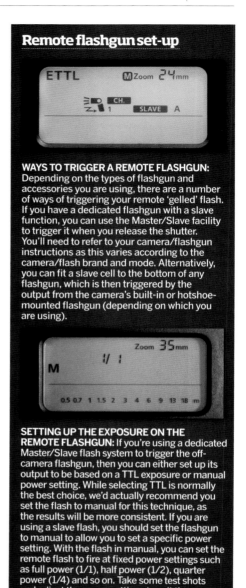

Remote flashgun set-up

WAYS TO TRIGGER A REMOTE FLASHGUN: Depending on the types of flashgun and accessories you are using, there are a number of ways of triggering your remote 'gelled' flash. If you have a dedicated flashgun with a slave function, you can use the Master/Slave facility to trigger it when you release the shutter. You'll need to refer to your camera/flashgun instructions as this varies according to the camera/flash brand and mode. Alternatively, you can fit a slave cell to the bottom of any flashgun, which is then triggered by the output from the camera's built-in or hotshoe-mounted flashgun (depending on which you are using).

SETTING UP THE EXPOSURE ON THE REMOTE FLASHGUN: If you're using a dedicated Master/Slave flash system to trigger the off-camera flashgun, then you can either set up its output to be based on a TTL exposure or manual power setting. While selecting TTL is normally the best choice, we'd actually recommend you set the flash to manual for this technique, as the results will be more consistent. If you are using a slave flash, you should set the flashgun to manual to allow you to set a specific power setting. With the flash in manual, you can set the remote flash to fire at fixed power settings such as full power (1/1), half power (1/2), quarter power (1/4) and so on. Take some test shots and adjust the power settings to suit the scene. Adjust power if you want a stronger or weaker effect or if you switch colour gels, as some absorb more light than others.

1 Here's our subject photographed using only our hotshoe-mounted flashgun. She's well exposed but the background is drab and dark.

2 We've set up a remote flashgun behind her, which fires to light the wall in the background but the effect isn't particularly attractive.

3 We've fitted a Lumiquest red gel and the colour adds interest, but, with the remote flash set to TTL, its output isn't as strong as we'd like.

4 Setting the remote flash to manual power provides a far stronger output, although the full-power 1/1 setting is far too strong.

5 We try various manual power settings to see which provides the best result and find that for this set-up, half-power works best.

Final image
While the red gel is attractive, it proves overpowering, so we try various colours and find green works the best.

Using slow-sync flash

Taking your camera off its default flash setting and selecting the slow-sync facility can greatly improve your flash exposures

Your digital SLR is set up to give great results in a wide number of picture-taking situations, and while it has a high success rate, often the results captured aren't quite what you had in mind. A perfect example with flash photography is when you take a night portrait on holiday, with the intention of capturing someone in front of an interesting building or scene. If you shoot using program or Full Auto mode, the camera sets a fast enough shutter speed so that shake is avoided and fires the flash to ensure the subject is well exposed. However, more often than not, the result isn't quite what you hoped for and while the subject looks OK, the scene behind is very dark, with only highlights like street lights showing up. It's a common problem with holiday snaps in particular, for instance when a night portrait set against the Eiffel Tower doesn't capture the scene quite as well as intended.

This is because while the selected shutter speed isn't a problem for the flash exposure, it is too short to capture ambient illumination correctly due to the low-light levels. The solution is to set your flash so that it fires in slow-sync mode, which in effect is firing the flash as normal, but selecting a slower shutter speed so that the longer exposure records detail in the scene. How you set slow-sync depends on the brand and model of camera you use, so check our table on the introduction spread for details. In general, with Nikon, Pentax, Olympus and Sony DSLRs, you need to set the flash mode to slow-sync and we'd recommend you try using program, shutter- or aperture-priority mode. Canon DSLRs don't have a slow-sync flash mode, instead you set aperture- or shutter-priority mode and the flash exposure takes care of itself.

If you're shooting a moving subject or a scene with moving subjects, it's worth bearing in mind that you can also set second-curtain sync, so that the flash fires at the end of the exposure rather than at the start. By doing this, any motion recorded by the ambient light during the exposure is captured before the subject is frozen by the flash. This gives a more natural-looking result as trails appear behind the moving subject rather than in front of it.

One word of caution: you'll be relying on longer exposures, so it's important you mount your camera on a tripod to avoid shake.

Fire, rotate, then flash!

The general technique for using slow-sync flash involves keeping the camera steady to ensure the shot remains shake-free. However, as with every rule of photography, they're there to be broken! By rotating the camera during the exposure, it's possible to produce some very unusual effects. Basically, you set a long exposure, then rotate the camera clockwise or anti-clockwise so that the ambient light records as a swirl, while the flash freezes the subject. Varying exposure times has an effect on the length of the trails of ambient light, so experiment: we would suggest that you start with a shutter speed ranging from 1/4sec to one second. Regularly view your images on the LCD screen and adjust accordingly.

1 Here's the scene captured using only ambient light in program mode. While the scene is well-exposed, the subject is slightly blurred due to the long exposure and looks off-colour as she is lit only by the tungsten street lamp. Exposure: 0.3 seconds at f/4 (ISO 320).

2 With the camera still in program mode, the flash is popped up, which automatically increases the shutter speed to avoid camera shake. The subject is now far better exposed but the background is much darker. Exposure: 1/30sec at f/4 (ISO 320).

3 The exposure mode is set to shutter-priority to allow slow-sync flash to have effect. A very long shutter speed of one second is set to show the effects of how subject movement during the exposure can ruin the image. Exposure: One second at f/7.1 (ISO 320).

4 With the camera still in shutter-priority, a shorter shutter speed of 0.3 seconds is selected, which is short enough to eliminate evidence of subject movement but enough time for the ambient light to record the scene. Exposure: 0.3 seconds at f/4 (ISO 320).

Slow-sync
Using slow-sync flash is a relatively easy way to ensure that outdoor portraits capture more of the scene's detail.

Use your ISO rating!
When selecting exposures, don't forget you can change the ISO setting as well as shutter speed and aperture to help you get the result you're looking for

ISTOCK PHOTO

Get the kids in a spin!

LUKE MARSH:
Ah, summer! As if it wasn't hard enough to get you kids to sit still for five minutes to have their picture taken, out pops the sun to whip them into a 'fresh-air' fuelled frenzy. Unless you're shooting at ridiculous high speeds, while constantly on the move, you may as well forget about capturing amazing summer family shots and switch to the still-lifes, right? Well, not necessarily. I got to thinking: 'what if I could combine a shot with a fun game my little boy is always nagging me to play – that's bound to keep him interested for more than the usual 30 seconds'. And that's precisely what I did. Any parent who's ever span around while holding their child will know that once you've started this game, be prepared for 'just one more time', for at least half an hour – plenty of time to get a great shot. Just don't try this straight after lunch, unless you've got a bucket handy!

Get ready!

TIME REQUIRED
30 MINUTES

EQUIPMENT NEEDED
NIKON D80 WITH 18-70MM LENS

ALSO USED
TWO CAMERA STRAPS

Creating a body harness

My home-made harness consists of two camera straps. The first is the neck strap already attached to my DSLR, the second is a spare strap that goes around my back to prevent the camera swinging from side-to-side. The most important aspect of this make-shift body harness is getting the height of the camera via the neck strap right so that the subject is positioned correctly in the frame. I found that placing the camera in the tummy region gave the most consistent results. I attached the second strap to where the first strap meets the camera, making it tight enough to prevent major movement, but not so tight that it is uncomfortable or prevents me accessing the controls. You can also buy a ready-made harness from brands such as Op/Tech (www.newprouk.co.uk).

1 When choosing a location, remember that the background will be blurred, so you won't need to worry too much about clutter – often a busier background helps with the sense of movement anyway. A garden or local play park is ideal, as long as there's enough space for you to spin without posing a threat of injury to either your subject or innocent bystanders.

2 For this shot, I'm going to use the camera's self-timer function to fire the shutter. All DSLRs have a self-timer, with most having the option to adjust the delay time in the menu settings. Here, I set the timer to fire five seconds after the shutter release is pressed, allowing ample time to get a decent spin going once I've pressed the shutter button.

3 With my DSLR set to aperture-priority (A) mode, I select a setting of f/10 for two reasons. Firstly, as the subject will be moving constantly in relation to the camera, it should allow enough depth-of-field to give a better chance of a sharp result. Secondly, this aperture naturally gives a slightly longer exposure, ideal for capturing the background movement.

4 I set the lens to its widest focal length so I can capture both the subject and the background. With the subject at arms' length in front of me, I press the shutter release half way to pre-focus, then switch to manual focus (M) so the DSLR won't hunt around trying to focus. I now fully depress the shutter release, setting off the timer and signalling for me to start.

⚠ **Watch your dizzy rascals!**
This spinning technique will make you and your subject very dizzy, so it's a good idea to take a 30-second breather in between shots. Keep a watchful eye on young children while reviewing your images to ensure their safety, as the spinning will effect balance and awareness considerably. Remember, this is a fun technique!

Final image
To create a bit more movement in the background I lower the ISO from 200 to 100, lengthening the exposure time slightly while maintaining the depth-of-field. So there you have it – I tried out a fun new photo technique *and* have fun with my son. The perfect summer's afternoon!

5 The first attempts are promising, and whereas there's always an element of luck that dictates where the subject will be in the frame when the shutter fires, my positioning improves with each spin I try. What I do notice is that my moving subject is blurred during the long exposure. To resolve this issue, I pop up the DSLR's integral flash to freeze the action.

6 I set the flash mode to Rear Curtain-Sync, which fires the flash at the end of the exposure. Its ideal as the slow shutter speed captures movement in the scene while the flash helps freezes the action for a split-second. It's a major improvement and I continue shooting until I stumble across a composition I like or until the subject gets bored (or sick!).

Studioflash outfits

While newcomers may find studioflash intimidating, the truth is that using it isn't as difficult as you may think

Although there are various studioflash kits available, ranging in price from under £200 to several thousand, the fact is most of them have very similar characteristics and features, and so all follow similar operating principles. A studioflash head is basically designed to fire a burst of flash at a given power setting – the extra functions and accessories are all geared to allow the photographer more control of the flash output. Learning how a studioflash system works and how it can be controlled is something that can take years of dedication and experience, but thankfully, getting to grips with the essentials is relatively easy. Much like using ambient light, the key factor behind your success with studioflash is learning how best to control it so that your subject is lit the way you'd like it to be. The big difference between studio and ambient light is the level of control you have – you are able to fine-tune the lighting's intensity and direction, as well as the nature of the light falling on the subject, far more than you could ever achieve with available light. This makes it an incredibly versatile form of lighting, but, obviously, one that does need time to use properly. In this section of the guide, we cover the basic workings of a studioflash system and how the various attachments, such as softboxes and brollies, can be used to control how your subject is lit.

Anatomy of a studioflash head

The following anatomy illustration is based on the rear of an Interfit flash head, but most will have a similar set-up, with easy-to-use and well-labelled controls.

REAR OF LIGHT

You'll normally find controls on the rear of the head, but some models have them on the side, too.

1) SYNC SOCKET Most studioflash outfits are supplied with a sync lead, which connects your camera to your flash head, allowing the flash to fire when you press the shutter button.

2) SLAVE CELL This sensor detects any flash output, so if your camera is connected to one light in a multiple set-up, its output will trigger the slave cell on other lights, making them fire.

3) POWER SETTINGS A key function of studioflash heads is being able to adjust the power of the output. Basic heads have fixed power settings e.g. ¼, ½ etc, while most advanced heads have step-less variable settings.

4) STATUS LIGHTS/BEEPS Most heads have lights or beeps to indicate the head has sufficient charge to fire.

FRONT OF LIGHT

Removing the lighting attachment |will usually reveal two bulbs, each with different uses.

5) MODELLING LAMP This tungsten bulb remains switched on, to allow you to compose the image, focus on the subject and predict the flash effect.

6) FLASH BULB These provide the powerful flash output. Most brands have specialised bulbs to fit certain heads or studioflash series. They're very fragile, so handle them with care.

Setting up your DSLR for using studioflash

When you're ready to shoot with studioflash, the key things to do are to set the camera to Manual and set the correct flash sync speed

CANON EOS DSLRS

(1) Set the main control dial to M to select manual mode.

(2) Turn the input dial behind the shutter button and set the flash sync speed (1/200sec on most Canon DSLRs).

(3) Once you've taken a flash meter reading, press and hold down the +/- button, then turn the input dial to set the aperture you require.

NIKON DSLRS

(1) Set the main dial to M to select manual mode.

(2) Turn the dial behind the shutter button (or on the right corner of the camera's rear) and set the flash sync speed (1/200sec on most models).

(3) Once you've taken a flash meter reading, turn the input dial on the front of the hand grip to set the aperture.

OLYMPUS E-SERIES

(1) Set the main control dial on the top-plate to M to select manual mode.

(2) Turn the input dial behind the shutter button and set the flash sync speed (1/200sec).

(3) Once you've taken a flash meter reading, press and hold down the +/- button, then turn the input dial to set the aperture you require.

PENTAX K-SERIES

(1) Set the main control dial on the top-plate to M to select manual mode.

(2) Turn the input dial behind the shutter button and set the flash sync speed (1/180sec on most Pentax DSLRs).

(3) Once you've taken a flash meter reading, press and hold down the +/- button, then turn the input dial to set the aperture you require.

SONY ALPHA SERIES

(1) Set the main control dial on the top-plate to Tv to select shutter-priority mode.

(2) Turn the input dial in front of the shutter button and set the flash sync speed (1/160sec on most Sony DSLRs).

(3) Once you've taken a flash meter reading, press and hold down the +/- button, then turn the input dial to set the aperture you require.

⚠ **Too hot to handle!**
Flash heads heat up quickly, so take care not to burn yourself when swapping attachments. The metal mount, as well as the bulb, can get hot, especially when the modelling lamp is turned on

Getting started
A couple of studio lights and some practice is all you require to take professional-looking portraits.

Studioflash Q&As

Q How much should I spend on a studioflash system?
A We would recommend you start with a two-head system, with a softbox and umbrella being good starter attachments. After extensive tests, we found the £250 Interfit EX150 MkII and the £560 Elinchrom D-Lite 4 IT to be excellent budget studioflash outfits for beginners.

Q What advantages do more expensive outfits offer?
A General build quality and reliability will be better, but the key benefits are power, features and performance. More power is useful as you can set the lights up further away from your subject, while relative light loss from attachments like softboxes is reduced. You'll find that more expensive heads allow more control over flash output and faster flash recycling times.

Q Are attachments from different systems compatible?
A In general, different brands have their own fittings so aren't compatible. However, Chimera make speed rings for their softboxes, which are compatible with just about any system.
www.chimeralighting.com

Q How should I set up my DSLR to use studioflash?
A You will need to set it to manual mode as the metering system is only set up for ambient light. Set the shutter speed to the flash sync speed and the aperture to whatever the flash meter states.

Q How do I take an exposure reading with studioflash?
A Simply use a flash meter connected to a light via a sync lead. Once you've set up the lights, hold the meter in front of the subject's face, take a flash reading and set the meter's recommended aperture on the camera. Don't forget to ensure that the flash meter and DSLR are set to the same ISO rating!

Q How do I connect my DSLR to my studioflash system?
A The plug at the end of the studioflash sync lead connects to your DSLR's PC socket. If your camera hasn't got a PC socket, buy a PC adaptor (around £10) that slots on your camera's hotshoe and connect the lead to this. A more expensive option is to buy a wireless trigger that sits on your hotshoe and triggers a receiver on the flash head.

Lighting accessories

Your studioflash system is only as good as the lighting attachments you choose to use with your flash heads

Flash heads are designed to produce a high-power burst of light, but it's the lighting attachment that you have fitted to it that dictates the effect of the light on the subject. If you've ever looked into buying a studioflash system, you'll no doubt have seen the various types of attachments on the market, each having their own unique way of affecting the intensity and nature of the light that reaches the subject and/or the background. While most basic kits are often supplied with a simple brolly or two and spills, there are a huge number of optional accessories available, and getting to know which are best suited to your needs is important. In our comprehensive comparison set below, we have used the most common types of attachments available for most studioflash kit systems to give you a better idea of how each affects the light.

Other accessories

FLASH METER Attach the sync lead, hold the meter in front of your subject and press the button to take a reading to discover what aperture you need to set your camera to for a perfect exposure.

BACKGROUND There are a variety of backgrounds available, from plain to coloured patterns. As well as paper rolls that fit on frames, there are several collapsible backdrops that offer the benefit of portability.

HOTSHOE PC ADAPTOR If your DSLR lacks a PC socket, this inexpensive adaptor slips onto your hotshoe and can be connected to the sync lead to trigger the studioflash.

REFLECTOR Using a reflector to bounce light back onto part of the subject or background is an alternative to using an additional light. Silver is the most efficient, white provides a softer and more natural effect, while using a black reflector can really accentuate cheekbones!

Umbrella (Brolly)

Available in white, silver and translucent, a brolly is one of the cheapest options available. Silver is very efficient at bouncing light, white gives a soft, natural effect, while translucent brollies provide the most diffused light.

Softbox

A real favourite, as it provides a very diffused light that's ideal for flattering portraits. The larger the softbox, the softer the light it produces. The majority are square, but some are rectangular and thin (also called strip lights).

Beauty dish

Beauty dishes are often used, as you may expect, for close-up 'beauty' and make-up shots. They give off a very harsh light in the centre, which enhances make-up, but also highlights flaws on a subject's skin.

Spill (Spill Kill)

Often supplied with the flash head, spills provide a concentrated beam of light. With portraits, they're useful for lighting backgrounds, but quite harsh when aimed directly at a subject's face.

Flash meter readings
When using studioflash, make sure the white dome (invercone) on your flash meter is set over the sensor, so it takes incident light readings, which will prove to be the most accurate

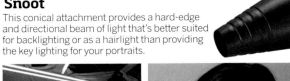

Lighting accessories
A quick look at a professional's studio provides an insight into the variety of attachments available.

Snoot

This conical attachment provides a hard-edge and directional beam of light that's better suited for backlighting or as a hairlight than providing the key lighting for your portraits.

Honeycomb grid

These provide a soft-edged circle of light and are a popular alternative to a snoot. They act in a similar way to a spotlight, but provide a wider spot effect. Honeycombs are available with various sizes of grids.

How to set studioflash exposures

If you want to use studioflash, you'll need to set your camera to manual mode. Paul Ward explains the three main methods to ensuring the correct exposure

FOR SOME PHOTOGRAPHERS, the first time they need to switch their DSLR to manual is when they want to use studioflash. That's because, other than the sync which triggers the flash, there's no information passing between the camera body and studioflash. It's down to you to set an ISO rating (usually a low 100 or 200), adjust the power of the studioflash, and set an aperture that gives a suitable exposure. The traditional (and best) way to match the studioflash output with the exposure is using a lightmeter that measures flash, but increasingly digital photographers are doing away with the separate meter and, instead, using the LCD monitor preview facility to work out the best settings via trial and error. Both methods have their good and bad points so either technique can be used. Here, we explain what they are and show you how to use these techniques for great studioflash photography.

Histograms

In other photography genres, the histogram can prove a useful tool in the search for a balanced exposure. When it comes to studio photography, Paul suggests it's better to avoid always relying on the histogram: "If you're shooting in a white studio, you're going to get big peaks on your histogram that will look odd, especially if you're used to interpreting a histogram of a landscape image. I think it's much better to judge the exposure on your LCD screen, or if you're shooting tethered, on your laptop." So, if you choose to use the histogram, be wary of overexposed peaks.

Get connected!

Your camera needs to be connected in some way to the flashheads before they can communicate and be told when to fire. There are a number of ways to achieve this and there is a solution to suit all budgets. The cheapest and most simple way to link camera and flash is with a sync cord. Costing around £10, the lead plugs in to the camera's PC socket at one end and the flash at the other and is very reliable. However, the main drawback is that the photographer is tethered to the flashhead, so mobility is limited. A more flexible method is to use an infrared system. A trigger is placed on the camera's hotshoe, while a receiver plugs into the flashhead's sync cord socket. No wires mean the photographer can wander freely around the studio, but infrared systems can be unreliable if the trigger and receiver are not in sight of each other. They are more expensive than a sync lead, but models from brands like Hama and Hahnel start at around £50.

For the ultimate in flexibility and reliability, most professional photographers opt for a wireless radio

triggering system. Like infrared, the radio systems have a trigger and a receiver, but unlike the infrared versions they don't suffer from line of sight issues as they're triggered by a radio signal. This convenience costs more, with top brands like PocketWizard costing a small fortune. However, third party brands like Hahnel offer more affordable options – the Hahnel Combi TF costs just £60 and should meet the requirements of most photographers.

✅ Contacts

Hahnel: www.hahnel.ie
Hama: www.hama.co.uk
Seculine: www.intro2020.com
Sekonic: www.sekonic.co.uk

Studioflash: Why use manual?

There is a good reason why we use manual mode when using studioflash. If you connect to your flashheads with the DSLR set in shutter-priority (Tv) mode, the camera will then try to select a (far too large) aperture for you, resulting in an overexposed and blown out image. Similarly, if you've selected aperture-priority (Av) mode then you're likely to be rewarded with a blurry image as the camera tries to use a long shutter speed based on the ambient light level. Only in manual mode can you control both settings to achieve a balanced exposure using flash.

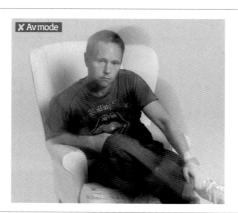

Know your flash sync speed!

It's important to know your camera's flash sync speed (X-sync), because if you exceed it, you will be blighted by a black bar covering a portion of the image, which is actually the camera's moving shutter curtain preventing the light reaching the whole frame. You can select a shutter speed slower than the maximum shutter speed. Paul tends to keep his camera set a 1/125sec. Here are the typical shutter speeds for big brand digital SLRs:
Canon: 1/200sec; **Nikon:** 1/250sec; **Sony:** 1/250sec; **Pentax:** 1/180sec; **Olympus:** 1/250sec.

Technique One: Trial and error

This system has a number of benefits. Firstly, you don't need to buy a lightmeter, so you've instantly saved money, and because you see the image on the LCD monitor an instant after firing the shutter, it's a very fast method to use. If the image is bleached or too light, it's overexposed, so you need to lower the ISO and/or select a smaller aperture. If it's underexposed, the image will be too dark, so you'll need to select a wider aperture and/or raise the ISO rating. Once you've selected a good exposure, you can choose to use the histogram to fine-tune the exposure by adjusting it in one-third or one-half stops.

The main drawback of this technique is that it's not as accurate as using a meter and you're relying on the quality of the LCD monitor for accuracy. In truth, so long as you know how to read a histogram – mindful of the advice on the left – you'll get a good exposure. The downside is that when using two or more flashheads, you're not getting the benefits of metering each light separately (see next page).

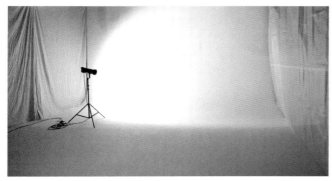

1 I position my lights depending on the look I want the image to achieve. I then take an educated guess at the exposure settings – in this case 1/125sec at f/20 (ISO 160) – and capture a test shot.

2 My camera's LCD screen allows me to review the test shot, which is far too dark. This is because my aperture of f/20 is much too small, and is not allowing enough light into the camera. Time to adjust my settings.

3 I change my settings to a much larger aperture of f/5.6, but this time I have the opposite problem and I have overexposed the image. You can see that highlights on the skin are what we call 'blown out'.

4 It's third time lucky as I change my settings to select an aperture in the middle of the two previous results (f/11) and I am rewarded with a balanced exposure that is neither under or overexposed.

Manual for studioflash: Using a lightmeter

There are a number of ways you can use a lightmeter to ensure your images are correctly exposed. Some take longer than others and, as we showed on the previous page, you can choose to ignore the lightmeter altogether. Lightmeters vary hugely in cost, but prices have fallen in recent years and around £100 will buy you an effective, brand new lightmeter. Brands to look out for are Sekonic, Gossen and Kenko

Ideal for less experienced photographers

Technique two: Take a reading with all lights on

Most amateur photographers – and many pros in fact – use this method to determine studioflash exposures. By taking a single exposure reading with the meter pointing away from the subject and towards the camera, you can quickly take a single meter reading that should give a correct exposure. It's a method that works really well, as you can view the result, then adjust the various power settings on each flashhead, take another meter reading and set this new exposure setting. It's a less involved method but judging the lighting balance isn't as straighforward – it can also be difficult to judge how each light individually illuminates the subject. Paul shows us how it's done...

1 I make sure the camera is in Manual mode and then dial in my ISO (160) into the lightmeter so it can calculate an accurate reading.

2 I then take a single reading from an area close to Kate's face. The lightmeter tells me that I should dial in an aperture of f/11 to achieve correct exposure around Kate's face so that's exactly what I do.

3 With the subject exposure taken care of by the lightmeter, all I have to do to make the background darker or lighter is to adjust the power setting on the head pointed towards the background.

4 After balancing the background exposure by adjusting the power settings, I'm able to achieve a correctly exposed image of my model, Kate. After some cleaning up in post-production, the image is complete.

Technique Three: Individual light readings

This is the method used by pros looking to get the best possible lighting effect. It involves using a lightmeter to take an individual exposure reading from each flashhead, allowing for very precise control of how each light falls on the subject to give the best possible lighting effect. It's the most involved technique, so takes a little more time and effort, but if you want to master the craft of studioflash lighting, it's one you should keep practicing at, as it's the method used by the masters of lighting, as it allows such fine control.

1 (Far right) With my lights set up and turned on, I'm ready to go. Note that I have put a diffuser in place to bounce some light back into Kate's face.

2 (Right) Input the ISO you've set on your DSLR into the lightmeter before you start – in this case, I used ISO 160. Make sure the lightmeter is in flash mode – usually indicated with a little lightning symbol. By doing this, the lightmeter will wait until the flashheads are fired before telling you which aperture you should set on your DSLR.

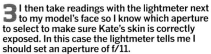

3 I then take readings with the lightmeter next to my model's face so I know which aperture to select to make sure Kate's skin is correctly exposed. In this case the lightmeter tells me I should set an aperture of f/11.

4 I take a reading next to the background, which tells me that I should set f/16. This smaller aperture tells me that, using f/11, the background will be bright, and help me create a high-key effect with the backdrop.

5 By taking multiple readings, I'm able to carefully control both the foreground and background exposures, resulting in a perfectly exposed final image. You can also use this to balance two lights aimed at your subject.

Studio set-up: One light

The most basic studio set-ups involve using just one light, so here are five techniques to get you started

If you want to learn how to control your lighting, you're best off starting with just one light. It's more than sufficient to produce stunning results and many great photographers still use a single head for their work. After all, outdoors we only have a single light source – the sun – so one light can deliver all we need. This set-up is very easy to control and the smallest adjustment to the light on your subject has a clear effect. This forces you to fine-tune the light's angle and diffusion method. And while you'll only have one source of illumination, you can also use reflectors in your set-up to bounce light and fill in any shadows.

The set of images below shows what happens when you position your single light (and softbox) at different heights and angles. As you can see, it's crucial that you learn the do's and don'ts of how to set up your single studioflash head to avoid some of the unflattering results shown below.

As mentioned earlier, you need to set your DSLR to manual mode and set it to the flash sync speed (if you don't know it, use 1/125sec as a safe bet or check your camera's manual). The aperture is determined by the meter reading you take, which is easy to do with a one light set-up. With the sync lead from the light attached, hold the meter in front of the subject's face and press the button to fire the flash and take a reading. Adjusting the power setting on the flash head allows you to effectively change the aperture you work with to in turn achieve the depth-of-field you're after. Add power to set a smaller aperture and reduce power to use a wider aperture.

ONE LIGHT: All you need to get started is your DSLR and a single flash head. With a bit of practise, you will soon find yourself getting great results!

1) Lit from above

With the light positioned high above the model's head, you get a more natural-looking light, though the shadows can be rendered harsh under the nose and chin. For the best results, get the model to look towards the light. You could also ask her to hold a reflector to fill the shadows.

2) Lit from below

Placing the light lower than the model's head, pointing upwards will eradicate any unsightly shadows under the nose and chin. For best results get the model to look down towards the light, which as you can see also makes catchlights appear in the subject's eyes.

3) Lit from the side

Place the light to either the left or right-hand side of your model's face for a strong, directional light, keeping half of the face in shadow. To increase your chances of capturing the catchlights in your subject's eyes, it is important to make sure the light is far enough forward.

4) One light & reflector

By holding a reflector close to the face, on the opposite side from the light, you will be able to even up any harsh shadows, much like using a second head. The closer you place it to the model, the stronger the reflection will be. For this technique it definitely helps to have an assistant!

Tilt the head
When shooting portraits, especially of females, try asking them to tilt their head slightly. This adds an air of friendliness to the shot, making the image look far more relaxed

5) Classic one light set-up

This technique involves placing the light slightly above and to one side of the model – pointing at an angle of 45° to one side and down at 45°. The resulting lighting gives a nice natural look to the face and well-placed catchlights as well, for a really pleasing, flattering result.

Studio set-up: Two lights

When you feel ready, you can extend your creative options by introducing a second flash-head into the mix

Many kits come with two heads, so once you've mastered lighting subjects with a single light, experiment with a second one. Often, when shooting with a single light, a reflector is used to fill shadows and provide an even lighting for your subject, but, without an assistant, they can be difficult to position.

A second head can be used instead, with the benefit that you can control the power output and add attachments to diffuse or precisely focus the light. The second light is usually called the 'slave', and is triggered when it detects the flash from the primary flash head. Using two lights gives you much more scope for different scenarios: you can light the model from different angles, or aim one light at the model and the other at the background.

So how do you meter for two lights? The simplest way is to set up the lights how you would like them, then take a meter reading from the subject's face and take a test shot at the recommended aperture. You can then consider moving the lights' position, adjusting the light ratio between the two or changing the power. Whatever you decide to do, take another reading to see what aperture you need and fire another test shot. A more accurate way of taking a reading is to check the exposure of each light in turn (i.e. only one light on at a time) and make adjustments accordingly. This will allow you to control the balance of flash between the two lights more accurately, but is a more involved process, so we would recommend using the simplest method first and try the second method once you have a bit of experience behind you.

TWO LIGHTS: This is a typical two-light set-up. The lights are fitted with a softbox and an umbrella to produce a diffused flattering light.

1) Lit from above & below

This is a typical headshot set-up, with the key light at 45° to the subject to give the most flattering light. The second light fills the shadows under the chin. This technique works for almost any subject. Set the key light two stops brighter than the second light.

2) Lit from above & rim light

The key light is above and to the right of the model. The slave light is positioned behind the model, opposite the key light. This throws light over her shoulder, adding a touch of light to her cheek. It adds interest to the shot, and gives her face more of a three-dimensional feel.

3) Lit from back & front

Here, we have one light in front of the model to light her face, and another behind her to light her hair, adding a bit of shine to it. This works well if your model has silky or colourful hair, and is a technique commonly used for 'hair' shots used in magazine advertisements.

4) Butterfly lighting

This is an old-fashioned technique that is not used very much in contemporary photography. By placing both lights above the model, pointing down at a sharp angle, to cast the shadows on her face, you create an interesting 'butterfly' shape under the model's nose.

5) Lit from both sides

Positioning both lights in front of the model, yet off to the sides, is probably the most important two-light technique to learn. It helps to get rid of shadows and gives a very even light across the face. This is useful for eliminating wrinkles, so is commonly used for beauty and make-up shoots. This lighting technique works with just about any subject, and is seen as a 'safe bet' for studio portraiture.

Studio set-up: High-key lighting

High-key lighting is one of the most popular techniques used by contemporary portrait photographers, and it's surprisingly easy

For a number of years, commercial portrait studios have been making a fortune out of their 'modern-lifestyle' portraits, often taken with wide-angle lenses and almost always shot against a white background. For the technique to work, the lights need to be turned up so high that any skin flaws become bleached out. The term high-key, although meaning different things to different photographers, generally refers to images with a very low contrast ratio so there's little difference between the areas of shadow and highlight. The results look fresh and clean, and with a bit of experimentation, it is easy to achieve good results. The shadows you can see are so subtle that the skin often looks flawless without the need for much, if any, post-processing. You will probably find that a lot of modelling agencies use this type of technique for their models' main headshots, as it's flattering and hides a multitude of blemishes and imperfections.

Contrary to what many beginners to studio lighting believe, this is a very simple technique to set up, and could even be achieved using only windowlight and a single reflector. While a reflector and a single studioflash can also work, for the best results you should use at least two studio lights. In this part of the guide, we're going to show you how to create a high-key lighting effect for your portraits using a two-light and a four-light set-up from your budget studioflash outfit.

1) The four-light set-up

This involves two diffused lights pointing at the subject and two lights, with no attachments fitted, pointing at the background. The principle is simple: your subject needs to be correctly exposed, whereas the background should be so grossly overexposed that it's rendered as pure white. To do this, with the background lights off, set up the two main lights so that they illuminate your subject and work out the correct exposure. Then, switch on the background lights and ensure the power setting for them is two stops brighter or more than it is for the subject's lighting. Just remember to take care that the background light isn't so bright that it spills off the backdrop and creates flare that spoils the overall result.

2) The two-light set-up

For this you will need two lights and the corner of a room with white walls and a white ceiling. The first light will be behind you, angled upwards to light the back wall and the ceiling, while the second light is used to illuminate the model's face and add light to the foreground.

The idea here is to light the back wall so that it is overexposed. The light should then bounce off it, so it mimics the effect of a huge softbox. The other flash-head, on the opposite side, lights the subject's face (though a reflector could have been used instead to bounce light back onto her). For most high-key shots of this type, the background lights are usually around two or three stops brighter than the foreground light. An easy way to do this is to set up the backlight first, taking a shot to ensure it's overexposed. Then, put your subject in position and take another shot to see how well exposed their face is, adjusting the foreground light until the exposure is correct. One thing you might want to try is setting the lights on a low power. This will allow you to use a wider aperture for your shots, which result in nice, soft-looking portraits.

✅ Diffusion dilemma

For a high-key effect, you'll need to diffuse your lights as much as possible. To do this, you could use big softboxes or simply bounce the light off a white wall, which will have the same effect

Create a magical self-portrait makeover

CAROLINE WILKINSON: This unconventional bleached-white portrait is easy to achieve and would make a great montage with various facial expressions. The technique is fairly straightforward, but its success hinges on preparation. The eyes, eyebrows and lips need to be striking to make the effect work, so have your model pile on the make-up and use a light-coloured powder to bleach the skin. As expected, the lads in the office weren't happy about applying red lippy and eyeliner, so I used myself as the subject. Although your model may look like a clown, the more make-up they apply, the better the final effect.

Get ready!

🕐 **TIME REQUIRED**
30 MINUTES

📷 **EQUIPMENT NEEDED**
NIKON D300, TRIPOD, ELINCHROM D-LITE 4IT WITH SOFTBOX

➕ **ALSO USED**
PHOTOSHOP CS4

Lighting set-up

SET-UP: Position one softbox above and in front of you, or your model, tilted down at a 45° angle. Start by setting the light to a mid-power setting, increasing or decreasing the power to get a balance between overexposing the skin, but not the lips, eyes or eyebrows, as they will form the basis of the picture.

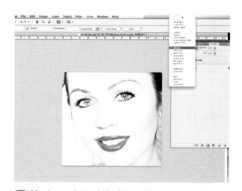

1 If you're shooting a self-portrait, you can use a remote release or if you haven't got one, your camera's self-timer. I opted for the interval timer as it allows me to continuously shoot a specified number of frames and it also adjusts the exposure, focus and metering before each shot. Check your DSLR's manual to find out if your camera has this facility and how to set it.

2 Position you or your subject on a stool and set the camera up so it aligns with the face. If you're doing a self-portrait, take a few test shots and reposition yourself, and the camera, until you're framed correctly. Then pull as many faces as you can for the frames set with your interval timer. Assess the pictures, adjust the light's power, reset the interval timer and re-shoot.

3 Having selected the best picture, open the image in Photoshop. As the only elements you'll need to form the picture are the facial features, select the Crop Tool and crop the image tight to get rid of any distractions. Now to boost the contrast, bleaching the skin further, duplicate the layer (*Layer>Duplicate Layer*) and change the Blending Mode to Overlay.

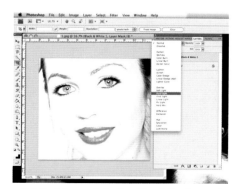

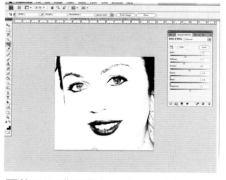

4 Adjust Curves to further bleach the face and darken the features (*Image> Adjustments> Curves*). Now flatten the image (*Layer>Flatten Image*). A clever way to boost contrast is to add a Black & White adjustment layer (*Layer>New Adjustment Layer>Black & White*). Click OK then click on the Black & White Layer on the Layer palette and set the Blending Mode to Hard Light.

5 Now, to adjust the intensity of certain colours. Click on the Layer Thumbnail (inset) in the Layers palette and tweak the colour sliders until the skin is nearly white and the features are at their strongest. Be careful not to turn the skin yellow. For this image I've taken the Cyan and Blue to -200 to enhance the eyes, Yellow to -27 to whiten skin and Red to -12 to boost the lips.

6 To get rid of any hair and the face's outline, go to *Layer>New>Layer* and select the colour white, then using the Paint Brush Tool set to a large soft brush get rid of the remaining outlines. Now if you want to make the canvas bigger to give more space around the features, use the Crop Tool to select the canvas, drag the squares to resize the canvas and then press Enter.

Final Image
My skin's never looked so flawless! This quirky take on a portrait will have everyone asking how you did it.

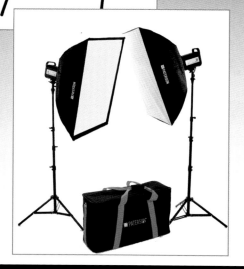
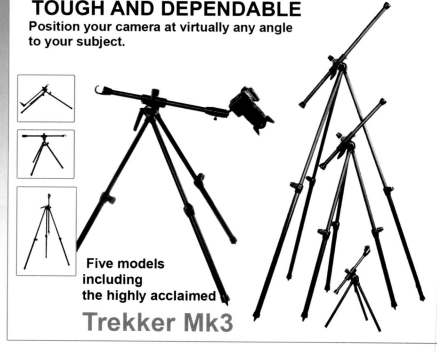

FAMILY PORTRAITS

IDEAS & INSPIRATION TO HELP YOU TAKE FAMILY PICTURES YOU'LL TREASURE FOREVER

The basic principles to photographing kids

Every child is unique and each has to be handled in their own special way. But there are certain steps to follow that can help you take your best ever pictures

IT ISN'T ALWAYS EASY, but capturing great shots of kids is one of the most rewarding moments in photography. Because they're often a law unto themselves, children often prove a real challenge to photograph. However, by learning a few basic skills and knowing how to make the most of their exuberant nature, you should be able to build up a nice collection of images. Strangely enough, when shooting kids, one of the key factors for success isn't anything to do with photography, it's actually all to do with how well you interact with the subject. It's essential that your subject feels comfortable and relaxed having their picture taken by you, otherwise they just won't look natural in the shots. Ideally, for at least the first ten minutes, keep any camera gear out of sight and spend the time chatting to the child and the parents. Only once they've got used to you should you think about getting out your DSLR and taking pictures. You'll normally find that younger children are generally the easiest to get on with and teenagers can be the most difficult, as they're more self-conscious about their image, and so often more reluctant to have their picture taken.

What sort of pictures should you aim to take?

Well, that's something that you, the parents and (in the case of shooting older children), the subjects themselves can decide. In the past, portraits were very formal and staged but thankfully things have moved on and the most pleasing portraits are those that capture relaxed subjects with happy and natural expressions. Shooting in the sitter's home is usually a very good starting point for various reasons. They'll obviously feel very comfortable in their surroundings and you'll also have the opportunity to have them change outfits or include different props, such as sunglasses, headbands etc if required. One more thing on clothing – don't get the children to wear their Sunday best as they won't feel comfortable, but instead have them dress in casual clothes or a favourite outfit.

As good as the home is, there is much to be said about heading out and shooting on location. Virtually anywhere is suitable – local parks, open countryside, industrial areas, beaches and city centres each have different attractions and moods that they can add to a portrait, so try as many as possible. And remember, there are countless ways to compose the subject in the frame, from head shots to full-length body shots and images where they're relatively small in the frame. The options are endless, so use your imagination and our expert advice to help you take your best ever pictures of children.

Vary your composition
As well as asking your subject to adopt different poses, you can dramatically alter your portrait by the way you frame your subject. Try close face crops, head and shoulders and full-length body shots.

How should you set up your DSLR?

When shooting portraits of kids, you'll need to be able to think on your feet and work fast, as while there will be moments where they're posing nicely, most of the time you'll be trying to keep up with their antics. Here's how we recommend you set up your DSLR

1) EXPOSURE MODE: The best bet is to use aperture-priority mode. We'd suggest you start off by setting f/5.6 and, to be honest, you can more or less leave it set to f/5.6 for the entire time. At this setting, you're working with a shallow depth-of-field that ensures your subject's face is sharp, but the background is thrown out of focus. What you'll need to keep your eye on is the shutter speed as you want to ensure it's fast enough to avoid shake. Increase the ISO rating (to a maximum of ISO 800-1000) when the shutter speed drops too low. Try to keep it at 1/200sec or faster and you should be fine if you're using a 50-200mm, or 1/300sec if it's a 70-300mm that you're using.

2) AUTOFOCUS: You can leave your camera set to multi-point AF mode if you want, but you run the risk of focusing on a shoulder, forehead, tip of the nose etc and not on the eyes, which is what you want to ensure is pin-sharp. We'd suggest you set your AF to single-point AF and use the central focusing sensor, which offers the best sensitivity. Set your AF mode to S (S-AF, AF-S) so that when you focus on the eye, you can lock the focus by pressing the shutter button halfway down, then recompose and take the shot.

3) METERING: Stick to multi-zone metering and you shouldn't have any problems. If your subject is predominantly dark, take one shot and check the LCD monitor, if detail is missing, add +1EV using the exposure compensation facility.

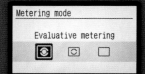

4) FILE FORMAT: Shoot in Raw for the maximum control over image quality and colour balance. However, when shooting fast sequences, it can slow your shooting rate because the buffer has to handle more data. Shoot JPEG only if you're not confident about converting Raw to JPEG or when memory space on your card is limited.

5) WHITE BALANCE: Ideally, set White Balance to suit the lighting conditions. If you're unsure what to use, set Auto White Balance (AWB). Bear in mind though, if you're shooting in Raw, you can easily change settings once you have the images on your computer.

The adorable nature of children means that you don't have to try and be too clever when taking their portrait. Make sure the lighting's good and the child is relaxed and you're almost there!

Keep it simple!

You'll see this tip emerge again and again, but the secret to great portraits is to try and keep everything as simple as possible, from choice of gear to lighting

BRETT HARKNESS

Photographing the kids: Be prepared

You can improve your chances of success by being ready in advance!

Get permission
If you're photographing other people's children, make sure you gain permission from one or both parents. Make sure to get a model release form signed too if you plan to have any published

WHAT KIT SHOULD YOU USE? Your choice of kit will largely be influenced by the type of pictures you're taking and the location of your shoot. If you're looking to shoot natural portraits and working with natural light, it's often best to keep your kit to a minimum – a DSLR fitted with a zoom, along with a reflector, is often all you need to capture a decent portrait. Sometimes you'll find you need additional lighting and while your camera's integral flash can provide fill-in, a hotshoe-mounted flashgun with bounce facility is better, while a basic studioflash set-up offers more scope for creative lighting. However, the more artificial lighting you add to a scene, the more effort you'll need to put into making sure the shots appear natural.

USING NATURAL LIGHT: From a beginner's perspective, working with natural light is a far easier proposition than having to use studioflash. But while there are not any power settings to twiddle with, there are still a number of factors that have to be considered when working with ambient light. For instance, the nature of daylight varies according to the weather conditions and time of day. On a sunny day, light is harsh and unflattering, on very overcast days it is dull, while shooting in the shade can give cool, flat results. By knowing how to control the various lighting conditions using a reflector, whether it's the gold, silver, white or black side, diffusers or flash, you can manipulate the light to help produce high-quality portraits. As you'll see mentioned time and again, a reflector is an indispensable accessory for virtually every form of lighting, while a diffuser is ideal for strong sunlight (see panel for details).

USING STUDIOFLASH: While daylight makes a fantastic source of portrait lighting, it's not always available when and where you need it. Being able to use studioflash offers you the chance to shoot when the weather's poor, at night, or when you're indoors. Using one or two flash heads with a brolly or softbox and a reflector can give you great results with minimal effort, once you've established how to position the lights and how to adjust the power of the flash heads. In the past, studioflash kits were usually only available to the wealthier amateurs and professionals, but there are now a number of kits available at very affordable prices that allows many amateurs the chance to try their hand at studioflash photography. And because you're able to instantly review your images on the LCD monitor, it's far easier to check lighting set-ups and make adjustments than ever before. If you decide that you would like to try out studioflash, then check out the studioflash sections of this guide for expert advice on the best studioflash kits, accessories and techniques to buy and try.

Natural light

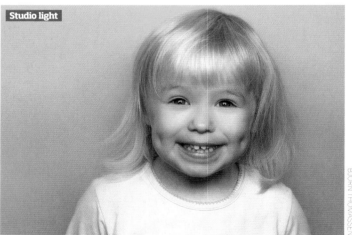

Studio light

Ideas for outdoor locations

Stuck for ideas on where to photograph great images of the kids? To be honest, almost any location is suitable, but here's a selection of tried and tested backdrops...

INDUSTRIAL AREA: Large corrugated doors, graffiti, warehouses with broken windows and skips have distinctive character. It may sound dodgy to some but we reckon its the perfect place to shoot some great portraits of the kids.

FARM: If you can visit a local farm and you're able to wander safely around it, you'll find that the barns, farmhouses, bales and general scenery can make for really interesting pictures.

PILLARS OR COLUMNS: You'll find the pillars and columns outside some museums, cathedrals and large libraries make great backgrounds. If you've more than one child in the scene, have them poking their heads around different pillars.

WEATHER-BEATEN DOORS: The texture of old wooden doors makes an ideal portrait backdrop. As well as brown, splintery wood, look for painted doors where the paint is old and flaky.

THE LOCAL PARK: Feeding ducks, sat on a bench munching sandwiches or enjoying an ice cream, sat beneath a tree shaded from the sun. The picture-taking possibilities are endless!

Lighting accessories

Ideal accessories to help you control and manipulate light are as follows:

REFLECTORS: A handheld reflector is a must. Ideally, go for one with a white side and a silver side. White reflects less light than silver but its effect is more subtle and natural. Silver is more efficient but should be used with care as its effect can be overpowering. Gold has a similar efficiency to silver but gives a warm glow, making it a good choice if your subject is a little pale or you're shooting in shade or on a cool winter day.

DIFFUSERS: These are worth considering if you plan to shoot outdoors in direct sunlight. Place a diffuser between the sun and subject to bathe your subject in a soft, diffused light that is ideal for flattering portraits. Diffusers are available in different sizes and diffusing 'strengths'. Some can be supported on stands but the majority are handheld, although you'll need a friend to assist as they're easily blown around in the wind.

Clothing

What your subject wears is important as it needs to fit in with the general mood of the image. Ask the pros their opinion on what children should wear and you'll get a variety of answers ranging from 'plain is best' to 'can't beat colours' and 'stripes are super'. Some base their choice on location or time of year. In other words, what's best is very subjective! However, what they all say is that your subject should feel very comfortable with what they're wearing and that for the majority of the time, casual clothing works best. So for boys, a pair of jeans and a T-shirt or fleece is good, while for girls, jeans and a blouse/T-shirt and cardigan is fine. Have them bring along a small selection of tops so that you get them to change outfits during the shoot. You should also give some thought to jewellery and props like hats and sunglasses.

Bright, beautiful babies

The arrival of a new member of the family is one of the main reasons people buy a DSLR. Follow our advice for some great baby shots!

FEW THINGS HAVE AS MUCH OF AN 'Aah' factor for cuteness as a baby. Those chubby cheeks, oversized eyes and toothless smiles are the perfect ingredients for wonderful portraits. However, as photogenic as babies are, they're not the easiest of subjects to shoot. For one, they're not going to pay any attention to what you're saying, so forget asking them to look out of the window or smile and thinking they'll oblige. Instead, expect lots of dribbling, snoozing, crying and looking everywhere except at the camera. Another obstacle you'll need to overcome, especially with babies just a few months old, is that they'll still not be strong enough to support themselves, so you'll have to shoot them lying down or being supported.

For that reason, many parents and family members are left frustrated that they can't capture the latest addition to the family as well as they'd like to. It's no surprise when you consider many get too close with a wide-angle lens and pop up the integral flash. The result is a distorted baby grimacing after the nth flash burst of its short life.

So, you've got a hard task ahead of you but there are several things in your favour. The first is that your subject isn't very mobile, so isn't going to run off anywhere. And because one or both parents will be present, they'll generally be comfortable and happy – especially if you plan to shoot after one of their regular naps or feeds.

Before taking any pictures, it's worth spending a few minutes with the baby so that they can get used to you. Talk to the baby, wave toys around, let them hold your finger, anything that puts them at ease. Make sure you smile a lot and don't feel daft for making silly noises or talking in a cutesy voice, it all works at establishing an initial bond.

If you're shooting indoors, aim to place your subject near patio/french doors; if outdoors, look for an area of well-lit shade. You'll want to work fast and be able to hand-hold the camera, so set a high ISO (400-800) and use a wide aperture. Look to shoot against as plain a background as possible – try shooting against light and dark backdrops, reviewing your LCD monitor to see which is most suitable.

A baby's eyes are relatively large in relation to the rest of their face so ensure at least one is sharply in focus. Change your viewpoint, shooting from above and then lying down to shoot from the baby's eye level or even lower.

Once you start taking pictures, you'll need to work fast. If you want, set the frame rate to continuous and shoot sequences whenever your subject is looking directly at you. You'll find the majority of images aren't worth keeping, but with any luck you'll get a handful of good shots that the parents will love. The better alternative is to leave the drive to single-frame advance and opt for less pictures taken with a little more craft and purpose.

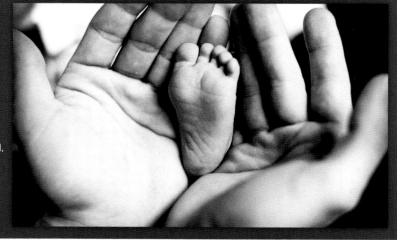

TOP: Young babies are often too weak to support themselves, so use furniture as an aid and, if possible, have a parent or assistant close by to prevent any accidents!

ABOVE: Be bold and try unusual compositions. Babies usually have very large eyes and so close crops and a very shallow depth-of-field allow you to emphasise this.

Top tips: Babies

1) GRAB THEIR ATTENTION You can usually get them to look at you if you hold a toy and give it a shake or a squeeze just before you plan to fire the shutter.

2) DON'T OVERDO IT! A ten-minute session is long enough. Take a tea break, then try again!

3) KEEP YOUR COOL You should not get frustrated or annoyed if the shoot's not going to plan. Accept that there's always the chance that you won't get any, let alone many, suitable pictures.

4) EXPECT MESS! Keep a kitchen roll handy for wiping away any baby-sick and some tissues for dribble or mucus from noses. Babies produce surprisingly large amounts of both!

5) GET CREATIVE If the baby's not looking at the camera, try unusual angles and compositions that might make a good shot, or concentrate on shooting hands, feet or other small details.

Hands & feet

You should make sure you take some shots of the baby's hands and feet. This is a good picture to try when the baby is only a few days old as they'll be sleeping most of the time and their wrinkly skin adds to the effect. Use soft light and keep colours pale and neutral, set a wide aperture for shallow depth-of-field and experiment with different angles and viewpoints. Try images in colour and black & white.

Baby behaviour
If you're very patient, you may be able to catch a moment when the baby is messing around and looking straight at the camera! Exposure: 1/500sec at f/4.5 (ISO 500).

✓ Convert to b&w
Bear in mind that baby pictures are ideal for conversion into black & white, so you should always consider turning some of your favourite shots into much-loved monochome images

Photographing toddlers

The early years of childhood, when a baby finally finds its feet, are exciting times for both parent and child, so be ready to capture these special moments with your DSLR

IF YOU HAD TO SUM UP TODDLERS IN ONE WORD, it would most likely be 'unpredictable'. From the moment that babies discover the mobility of their own two wrinkly little feet, they're up and about with a mind of their own, exploring a whole new world. It's something that they'll continue to do for a number of years, so you've plenty of time to get some great shots of them in their first years of discovery. That said, kids grow up extremely quickly at this stage of life, so you don't want to miss out on never-to-be-repeated moments. You need to be prepared for anything they're likely to do, so if they pull a face, fall over, break into fits of giggles, or anything else that kids of this age often do, you'll have your camera ready to capture every treasured moment.

It's really important that you spend a bit of time getting to know the kids and more importantly, give them a chance to get to know you too. If you're photographing your own kids or your family or friends' children, this isn't such an issue, but if it's a child you don't know, imagine how they'll feel if a complete stranger starts taking their photos. Spend ten to 15 minutes in the company of the parents chatting to the child and gaining their trust and you'll find that they're far more relaxed and responsive.

A telezoom like a 50-200mm is without doubt the best choice of lens, as you can shoot at a distance without your subject even knowing that they're being photographed, allowing them to behave completely naturally. If your images aren't completely candid, make sure that you spend a little time playing games and talking to your subject before you start taking pictures, so that they get used to you being around. They'll soon lose interest in you, allowing you to shoot more freely. Look to use a reflector if shooting indoors – you'll find many toddlers see the reflector as a large, fun, shiny toy, so if they're playing with it, aim for tight portraits while their faces are well lit! Remember not to carry around too much kit, it will get in the way and you'll invariably be switching lenses when the best photo opportunities happen!

You need to have a lot of patience when photographing young children. Don't try to manipulate them, if they decide that they've had enough of having their picture taken, then let them roam around for five minutes, and then try and coax them in to a few more shots. But always be ready. When the chance comes to grab a shot, your camera should be correctly set and you should be able to capture the moment before it's gone.

ABOVE: Allow toddlers freedom and it won't be long before they forget about the camera, allowing you to capture very natural candids.

LEFT: Always keep in mind that you can create sets of images that tell a story. Triptychs (a set of three images) are very popular and worth trying out.

Make the studio fun!

If you're using studioflash, it's not unusual for toddlers to get a little anxious, so find things that easily distract them. It's natural for parents to bring some toys with them, but you can have some of your own there too as young kids love to try out new toys. Contributor Bjorn Thomassen has another solution: "I've found that bubbles can really work at capturing their attention and they'll usually widen their eyes and smile when bubbles are near. I also have a Disney CD playing quietly in the background as these familiar songs help put them in a 'happy

Gift ideas

FRAMED PHOTO-STORY
Producing framed prints that are made up of a multiple of images is a great way to provide a photo-story of the day. You'll find many photo outlets and art stores, as well as some large department stores, sell frames with mounts for holding several images. It makes an interesting and eye-catching variation to the normal method of mounting a single image within a frame.

Top tips: Toddlers

1) MAKE THE SHOOT FUN!
The more the session is about
having fun and less about the
pictures, the better. The best
photo sessions are when you take
the kids' mind off what's going on.

2) CAPTURE BREAK-TIMES
Keep shooting even during the
'down time' when kids are taking
a break, having a drink etc, as
you'll get great candid shots.

3) LET KIDS DO THEIR THING
Keep giving instructions and
they'll soon get bored or upset.
Instead, allow them to do their
own thing and occasionally see if
you can prompt them to pose.

4) CHANGE THEIR CLOTHES
It's amazing how a quick outfit
change can give images a whole
new look and feel. Add a change
of location and you'll come away
with a real mix of images.

5) INCLUDE THE PARENTS!
Don't forget to get mum and dad
involved – even if they say no!

Timid toddlers
If your subject's shy, play
games with them, such
as peeking over chair
backs or around doors,
then grab the shot.
Exposure: 1/320sec
at f/3.5 (ISO 500).

Photographing youngsters

They can be precocious, naughty and downright cheeky. But at this age, kids are often at their most photogenic, too!

I T'S GENERALLY ACCEPTED BY MANY PARENTS that the most enjoyable years of childhood are when their kids are aged between five and ten. These are the years when children develop their personality and a small sense of independence, which can lead to some fantastic photographic opportunities.

In many respects, these younger years have the potential to deliver the best child portraits. Because the kids are able to run around and play on their own, you've got plenty of scope to capture some excellent candids. Fit a telezoom to your DSLR (50-200mm or 70-300mm are good options) and you can keep your distance so that your subject carries on oblivious to the fact that they're having their picture taken. After you've taken a few shots, a good idea is to find a good viewpoint, call their name and, with your DSLR set to continuous drive, rattle off a few frames when they look over.

A great benefit of kids at this age is that they're (fairly) responsive to instruction, so if you need them to sit, stand, turn around etc, they're more than likely to do so. This allows you to shoot a good mix of pictures, from candids to more staged shots, in a relatively short space of time. And, because your subject will start to get a little bored after a few minutes and begin messing about again, you can expect a few silly faces and poses towards the end of the session.

You should aim to be very relaxed about how you 'pose' your subjects. A good method to try is to ask them to stand/ sit by a particular place and then take a couple of shots. If they look tense, get them to shake their arms and head to get them to relax and laugh as they do this, so they feel like they're having fun. Take a couple more shots, tell them they're doing great and get them to raise/drop their chin, tilt their head and so on until you get the shot you're after. Try a variety of viewpoints and crops to really mix up the shots. And at the end of the shoot, tell them to go crazy for a couple of minutes and capture them at their least sensible!

Kids' fashion has come on in leaps and bounds so as well as head and shoulder shots, be sure to take some full-length body shots to include the fashion of the time. If they have a unique sense of style, use it and show it! It might be they like to wear hats, bright colours or dress up as Superman. Your ultimate goal should be to take a good mix of images that together captures various aspects of your subject's nature.

As always, if you can, have an 'assistant', (i.e. a friend or family member) handy as they can hold a reflector or diffuser to give you added control of the lighting.

Doorways are ideal for getting a youngster to stand or sit in front of and pose candidly for pictures. Choose clothes that suit the colour of the door and if the youngster's wearing layers of tops, get them to lose the fleece/ jumper after a bit and pose in their T-shirt. And we do keep saying it, but you can't beat the extra bit of light that a reflector can give.

GIFT IDEAS

Canvas blocks

They've been around for a few years but there is little sign of their popularity diminishing. Having a child portrait on a canvas block is a distinctive way of displaying your best shots and a great photo gift idea.

Inkjet prints

If you fancy producing your own range of photo art, then check out the wide range of fine art papers available to use with inkjet printers. Some good names and types to try are Hahnemuhle Photo Rag Satin Glossy Fine Art and Permajet Royal Fine Art.

Top tips: Youngsters

1) WORK QUICKLY
A telezoom (e.g. 50-200mm) allows you to quickly change the composition from tight head shots to full body shots.

2) ENSURE THEY'RE AT EASE
Before you start taking pictures, explain to them what you plan to do and get them to relax, as it will be easy and over with quickly.

3) BE POSITIVE! Constantly tell them they're a natural at having their picture taken and that they look really good in the shots. Even at a young age, kids will benefit from this encouragement.

4) LET THEM PLAY! If they start messing around, let them play and capture some candids, before stopping them to get ready for the next shoot.

5) REWARD THEM! A bribe (toy, sweets etc) always works a treat and a reward for their efforts will help them say yes again!

Photographing youngsters: Brothers Caleb & Miles at the farm

Daniel Lezano heads to a local farm with *Digital SLR Photography* reader Sean Norris and his two sons, Caleb (9) and Miles (6), to see what was possible in an hour at an unusual location that most parents wouldn't even consider for a portrait shoot

I'VE DRIVEN BY A LOVELY FARM on my way to and from work every day and always fancied shooting portraits there. So a week before the arranged shoot, I visited the farm to meet with the owner Harry to get his permission, rather than turn up unannounced.

Sean is a subscriber to *Digital SLR Photography* and is also a good family friend, so I know his two boys well. After discussing the shoot with him, he had a good idea of what I wanted to do and on arriving at the location, we left the camera gear in the car, and had a walk around to seek out potential spots to take our pictures. Within a couple of minutes, we'd earmarked a stone wall, some wooden doors, large steel containers, metal horse-boxes and hay bales as all potential locations.

It was a sunny day, so as well as a reflector, I took along a large Lastolite Skylite diffuser in case I had to work in direct sunlight. We started off using the brick wall as a backdrop, with Caleb and Miles standing in front of it or leaning against it. I tried a number of viewpoints, with my favourite being to shoot the wall at an angle, so that it vanished off into the distance. I also shifted Miles and Caleb, so that sometimes they were in contact with the wall, then moved them forward to put some distance from the wall to help throw it out of focus. As well as shooting from the kids' eye-level, I also knelt and lay on the ground to get different perspectives. I took a shot with no reflector, followed by a couple with the white then silver sides of the reflector (and occasionally the gold side), to see how this affected the light falling on the subjects.

Next, we took pictures against some metal tanks, which were bathed in bright sunlight. We rested a large diffuser against the tanks and had each of the boys stand beneath it in turn. After taking a number of portraits of the boys from different angles, we headed to the wooden doors and used the diffuser panel in much the same way to soften the light. We also tried shots against some horse-boxes parked in deep shade. Setting a high ISO of 1000 and a wide aperture, we used the silver and gold sides of the reflector to bounce some light back on to the boys. The lads were in a playful mood, so I didn't try to stop them and shot away as they messed about, before heading for the hay bales for the final shots of the day.

I took a series of images of the two boys on their own and together. We went through a variety of relaxed poses, from sitting to lying down and standing on the bales and captured some great shots. Again, relatively low-light levels meant care was needed to avoid camera shake and to make sure that the reflector was bouncing enough light onto the boys' faces. Despite using a very similar set of skills and techniques at each of the different shoots while at the farm, each of the backdrops had a profoundly different effect on the result. And don't forget, each of the shots are open to black & white conversion as another creative possibility. In an hour, I'd taken around 200 shots and, having reviewed the LCD monitor, knew there were several that would please their parents.

Gold reflector

Silver reflector

An hour is more than enough time to wander around a location and take pictures. Any longer and the youngsters will start getting bored. Remember to take a reflector (and if possible a diffuser) with you, but use the gold and silver sides carefully as their effect can be overpowering.

Youngsters: Summary

✔ Regular reassurance and praise will help nervous kids relax in front of the camera.

✔ You'll find a single location has the potential for several types of backdrop.

✔ Older brothers are less likely to want to 'cuddle' their younger siblings as sisters are.

✔ If you plan to use a large diffuser, make sure you have an assistant to help!

✔ Take care with gold and silver reflectors in bright sunlight as their effect can be overpowering.

Image details
All images taken in aperture-priority mode with autofocus set to single-point AF and multi-zone metering.

It's time for the teenagers!

Be careful not to call them kids – teenagers need to be treated like adults if you want to get the very best from them!

AS EVERY PARENT WILL testify, kids rapidly develop far more independence when they reach secondary school and each year as a teenager sees them develop both mentally and physically at a startling rate.

As a photographer, what this generally means is that your subjects will need to be treated more like adults than as children if you're going to have any chance of getting them to perform in front of the camera. So while you may want to offer some advice on what they should wear, for instance, don't be negative if they turn up wearing the complete opposite of what you've asked them to. Work with them and when you've taken a good selection of shots, ask them to change outfits and see if they'll go with what you want them to wear.

You'll generally find that they have a short attention span and act as if they have better things to do than have their picture taken. But if you're friendly, interested in what they have to say and listen attentively to ideas on how they want to be shot, you'll find it goes a long way to keeping them on your side. If you can get your subjects to enjoy what they're doing, you'll find them literally shift from pose to pose after every shot!

Kids are at their most self-conscious when they're in their teens and while some are pure exhibitionists, the majority are worried about how they'll look in pictures, especially if their hormones are playing havoc with their skin. Your aim should generally be to capture them in flattering light, make them look like 'grown-ups' rather than kids and try to get them to enjoy the experience

Teenagers can be real fun to work with, so try and capture this in your images. Have your assistant or a friend try and make them laugh and be ready to capture the moment. Many teenagers have strong interests so try and incorporate this into the image where possible, either through what they wear or what you include with them in the frame, e.g. a skateboard, car etc.

What do *they* want?

As well as a selection of pictures that you and the parents like, you should also make sure to ask the subjects how they would like to be shot. You may be surprised at what they come up with! When we asked Katie for ideas on how she'd like to be shot, she said she wanted a nice black & white image looking away from the camera and showed us a picture in a magazine. It wasn't the sort of picture we'd planned but we spent some time setting it up and capturing the sort of look that Katie wanted. For this image, we sat Katie next to some french doors so that she was side-lit by diffused light, then set up a studioflash with a small softbox on the floor to provide a little light from low down on the opposite side. The image was then converted to black & white using Photoshop.

Mono lighting

If you plan to convert images to black & white, it's worth bearing in mind that you don't have to worry about any colour casts from lighting.

Top tips: Teenagers

1) Make sure they're happy, relaxed and having fun. You'll end up with far better images than if they're bored and uninterested.

2) Ask them if they've any favourite photos of some of their heroes and see if you can shoot them in a similar style.

3) Give them a rough idea of what you'd like them to wear (e.g. plain T-shirt, jeans, etc) but make sure they're happy with your choice.

4) Try not to sound too formal when talking to them, but be careful not to use words like 'cool' if you think it could backfire!

5) When you've got a good shot, show it to them on the LCD screen. If they like what they see, you'll give them the needed interest to continue.

6) Don't shoot with their parents or friends watching as they'll probably feel intimidated, so ask those who aren't being included to leave the room!

7) Make sure to give them a small gift (e.g. £10 iTunes voucher) as a thank you and send them some prints of the best shots. It's a small price to pay for their time and will also mean they're more likely to say yes next time.

BRETT HARKNESS

Review your shots

Some teenagers worry how they look in the pictures, so after part of the shoot, run through the images you've taken on the LCD screen and show them the best ones to boost their confidence!

Teenagers usually enjoy a fashion portrait shoot as it allows them to pose in their favourite clothes. Make sure to produce some prints of their favourite shots as a 'thank you'.

A fun lifestyle shoot with teenage sisters

Daniel Lezano sets out with two sisters for an outdoor photo session. As he discovers, if they're having plenty of fun, it's not difficult to capture lots of great shots!

HAYLEY (16) AND KATIE (14) ARE PART OF my extended family and I've known them for around ten years. They're no strangers to having their pictures taken by me, often for various features in the *Digital SLR Photography* magazine, but this was the first time they'd been asked to pose 'as themselves', rather than to show specific techniques or as part of a camera test. A few days before the session, I had asked them how they wanted to be shot and they didn't really have any clear ideas, so I asked them to have a look through various fashion titles and back issues of *Digital SLR Photography* to see if any type of portraits took their fancy. They came back with plenty of ideas, ranging from nice black & white portraits to a 'fashion lifestyle portrait' similar to the type taken by contributors Brett Harkness and Bjorn Thomassen. As for their parents, the request was simple – produce a nice deries of images of the two of them together.

I had already scouted out a location full of character in the centre of their home town, Stamford in Lincolnshire and on the day, the overcast conditions were ideal. A set of large blue doors provided the ideal backdrop to take some 'fashion portraits' of Hayley. First though, we asked the two sisters to mess around a bit and make the whole photo experience more fun. I snapped away while they pulled faces, pushed each other about and gave each other piggybacks and after a couple of minutes, they realised the shoot had the potential to be lots of fun, so they were lively and responsive to my instructions. I shot the two of them leaning against each other, hugging and so on and the results were excellent, as the two of them looked like they were really enjoying themselves!

Next, it was time to shoot Hayley on her own. Running through a few poses and shooting from various angles resulted in several nice shots within minutes. The silver side of the reflector was ideal for bouncing light on to Hayley and filling in unwanted shadows. I asked Katie to hold the reflector to keep her involved and interested. As well as full-body poses, we took some head and shoulders shots and tight crops of her face. During the shoot, I tried to let things flow with minimal interruptions, but kept an eye out for small details, asking Hayley to move stray hairs away from her eyes and also removing her pink necklace. We also added a bit of fun to proceedings by having Katie use the reflector as a makeshift fan, blowing Hayley's hair in all directions while I fired away. The results were very hit and miss as her hair was flying everywhere, but it kept their enthusiasm high, which was important as I still had more shots to take. With both very relaxed, I took some more of the two of them together by a blue door, this time with an assistant holding the reflector. In the space of only 20 minutes, we had captured a real mix of pictures and having reviewed them on the LCD screen, it was pretty clear that there were several images from the shoot that could be printed and framed.

Have some fun!

If the subjects are having fun, you're going to get great shots. I left the two to mess about, grabbed some shots, then when they were totally relaxed, asked them to give me a few nice poses. Using the reflector as a makeshift fan kept their spirits (and Hayley's hair) flying high, too!

GIFT IDEAS

Floating panels

A modern and stylish way of displaying images is to have them made into a floating panel. The image is printed and placed on a thin sheet of lightweight aluminium, which when mounted on the wall using its batons (inset) appears to be 'floating'. Our sample was supplied by *Studio 100 Artwork* and proved to be very high quality, with strong colour and excellent detail. They produce floating panels in various sizes.
For further details, call 01252 712 630 or email: studio100artwork@aol.com

Photo books

A number of firms offer photo books made up of your pictures and text. We made our own using *Apple iPhoto* software, then paid for it online and a week later, it had arrived in the post!

Hayley & Katie

Teen shoot: Summary

✔ Formal settings are nowhere near as much fun as the outdoor for a lifestyle shoot. The latter is also far better for revealing more of the subject's personality.

✔ Having two (or more) teenagers together means they have more fun during the session and this makes for much better pictures. And when each is being shot on their own, the other can be kept involved by assisting with holding the reflector.

✔ Don't believe the stereotype of teenagers as grungy, sulky and introverted. Most are intelligent, streetwise and fun to photograph.

✔ Before the day of the shoot, be sure to mention make-up if you're photographing girls. Make sure they only apply a small amount to cover blemishes and don't go over the top!

Image details
Exposure: 1/400sec at f/4.5 (ISO 250).

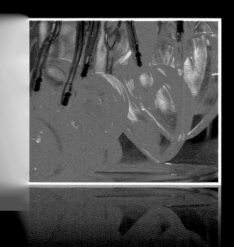  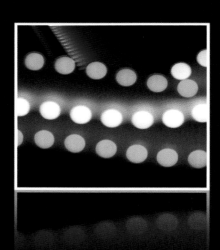

DIGITAL TECHNIQUES

IMPROVE YOUR IMAGES & ADD CREATIVE EFFECTS WITH OUR POST-PROCESSING TUTORIALS

Give your portraits a perfect digital makeover

IAN FARRELL: The subject of digital retouching in portraits, fashion and advertising photography always provokes mixed reactions. Some think it's unnecessary and over the top, while others think that digital post-production is the making of a photograph. One fact, however, is undeniable: you won't find a commercial shot in a magazine or advert that hasn't been retouched. Editorial photography is so routinely touched up that it's now the norm. Eyes brightened, teeth whitened, skin smoothed and blemishes removed. And if you are looking at a glossy magazine right now and can't tell, it just means it's been done really well.

The secret to doing this type of retouching is to take your time and be as precise as possible. Use a graphics tablet and set aside an hour for a single image. The Photoshop techniques themselves are actually quite simple, it's just the way in which they are applied that is important. Let's have a look what's involved.

Get ready!

⏱ **TIME REQUIRED**
60 MINUTES

📷 **EQUIPMENT NEEDED**
ADOBE PHOTOSHOP
CS OR ELEMENTS

➕ **ALSO USED**
GRAPHICS TABLET

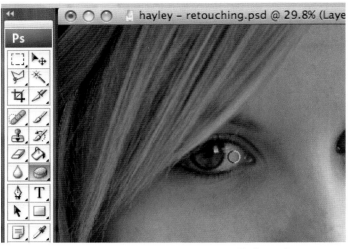

1 Eyes can be brightened to add impact. Use the Sponge Tool set to Desaturate, which you'll find in the tool box under the same square as the Dodge and Burn tools. Select a small, soft-edged brush at an opacity of 20%, go over the whites of the eyes removing colour. We've deliberately oversaturated the eye on the left to show how effective this tool can be.

2 Everyone has wrinkles, spots and pimples, even supermodels. These are easily removed with the Clone Stamp Tool or Healing Brush Tool, and it's best to do this on a separate layer to avoid spoiling the original image. Create a new working layer by clicking *Layer>New>Layer*. Whether using the Clone Stamp or the Healing Brush Tool, start with the opacity around 15% and build it up.

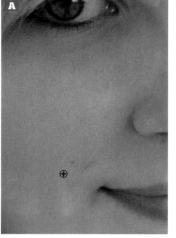 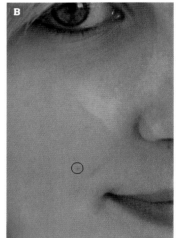

3 Select the Clone Stamp Tool and find an area of clean skin near to the spot you want to improve. This is important as it will most likely have a similar tone. Holding *Alt* will make a crosshair appear. Click on the clear area before moving the mouse over to the pimple. Then position your cursor circle over the pimple, hold the mouse down and slowly 'paint' over the area until it fades.

4 With the obvious skin blemishes removed, it's time to smooth out the rest of the texture in the skin. We'll go overboard first, then pull some of the original texture back to make things look more natural. Start by merging the layers by selecting the original image, the cloning and healing edits and then clicking *Layer>Merge Down*. Then duplicate the layer (*Layer>Duplicate*).

5 Apply some blur to this duplicated layer using the Gaussian Blur filter (*Filter>Gaussian Blur*): 10-15% should do it. The next step depends on which software version you are using. If you use Elements then you need to erase portions of the blurred layer so it only shows on your model's skin. Use a soft-edged brush and take your time. This is where a little bit of patience will really pay off.

Original

ABOVE: The original image was shot with the model's face illuminated by soft daylight, although these techniques are equally applicable to pictures taken outdoors or with sources of artificial light such as studioflash.

Clone tool & healing brush

As you can see from Step 3, the Clone Stamp Tool is great at copying pixels from one part of the image and pasting them on to another. But what is the Healing Brush Tool and what situation is right for each tool? The Healing Brush Tool also allows you to fix blemishes, but this time the tool takes clean pixels from around the area you're attempting to fix and pastes them over the problem, trying to match the texture, lighting and shading for a more natural look. So, if you're just trying to erase something from your image, try the Clone Tool, but, if you are working on something more detailed, the Healing Brush is best.

Final image

Specialist software
Photoshop isn't your only option for retouching images. Check out other packages such as the excellent Portrait Professional (www.portraitprofessional.com), which costs only £65!

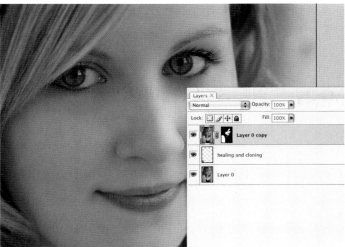

6 If you are using the full version of Photoshop, a much more elegant solution is to add a layer mask (*Layer>Add Layer Mask>Hide All*), which will hide the blurred layer. You can then paint the blur back on to the skin by clicking the mask icon in the Layers palette and using Photoshop's Paint Brush Tool to apply white paint. To remove blur, switch to black paint.

7 Whichever method you choose, you will end up with an over-the-top result. Throttle this back by decreasing the opacity of the blurred layer, which will let some of the original shine through. How much to adjust this control depends on the picture you are working on, so feel free to experiment. It's important to give you subject's skin some texture or it will look very odd.

Boost contrast with blending modes

CAROLINE WILKINSON: Manipulating contrast and colour saturation is what Adobe Photoshop excels at, but these two properties are often interlinked. Boost an image's contrast and you'll notice the colours may look oversaturated too. While adjusting the Levels or Curves is the most common way to change contrast and the Hue/Saturation tool for adjusting colour, using blending modes in a multi-layered image can be quicker and give you more creative flexibility.

Put simply, blending modes determine how a top layer interacts, or 'blends' with the layer underneath. There are 25 blending modes to pick from, each having a different effect, but there is also a group dedicated to changing contrast, including Soft Light, Hard Light, Linear Light, Hard Mix and, one of the most used, Overlay. Each one handles light and dark differently – so it's worth experimenting – and it's worth noting that you can add them to any layer: a duplicate layer, an adjustment layer, a fill layer or a different image layer.

If you are new to working with multiple layers and blending modes, don't be daunted, this may sound advanced but it's not. In fact, this tutorial could be the encouragement you need to start using layers in all of your Photoshop and Elements editing. Let's see how it's done.

Get ready!

⏱ **TIME REQUIRED** TEN MINUTES

📷 **EQUIPMENT NEEDED** ADOBE PHOTOSHOP OR ELEMENTS

Finding Layer Blend Modes

While you can go to *Layer>Layer Style>Blending Options* and find the Blend Mode drop-down menu under General Blending, along with many other advanced options that will look very confusing to you at this stage, there's a much quicker way. All the blend modes can be found on a drop-down list in the top-left corner of the Layers palette, which by default will have Normal blend mode selected.

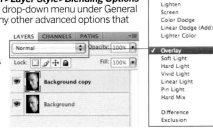

1 You need at least two layers for this technique to work, as a blend mode determines how a top layer interacts with the layer underneath it. So, to begin with, I duplicate the Background Layer, by clicking the layer and choosing *Layer>Duplicate Layer* or *Ctrl+J*.

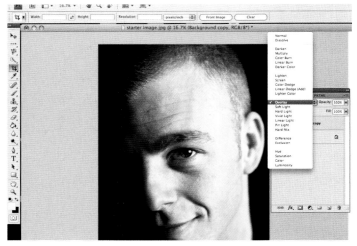

2 I want to boost the contrast, so I run through the list of blend modes and finally opt for Overlay, as it darkens the blacks and lightens the highlights. If the effect is too strong, try reducing the top layer's opacity. By boosting the contrast, however, I've oversaturated the face, making it red.

3 I need to separate the contrast and saturation, so sticking with Overlay and at opacity 100%, I take the colour out of the top layer using the command *Image>Adjustments>Desaturate*. It's given me the boost in contrast I want and muted the colours. I like it!

4 By desaturing the shot, I've lost the colour in the eye. To give it back its impact, I have used a Quick Mask and small brush to select the eye on the Background Layer. Click the Quick Mask icon again to reveal marching ants. I then boost the colour (*Image>Adjustments>Hue/Saturation*).

Quick fix

Overlay is a combination of Multiply and Screen blend modes. Use them separately to darken or lighten images, respectively. Great if you're dealing with over or underexposed photos

Final Image

Overall, I'm happy with the final image, but thought it was a bit soft, so I added a High Pass filter to boost the detail. I did this by duplicating the Background Layer again, and making it the top layer, then adding a High Pass filter (*Filter>Other>High Pass*) set to 5 pixels and selecting the blending mode to Overlay. Experiment with different filters and blending modes for various creative effects.

Original

Give your favourite portrait a 1950's style makeover!

CAROLINE WILKINSON: When someone says Andy Warhol, probably one of the first images to pop into their head is a colourful montage of Marilyn Monroe or a Campbell's soup can. Warhol is one of the most recognised artists of the 1950's pop art movement and we're still replicating his style 60 years later, with a lot more ease since the introduction of Photoshop. When it comes to picking an image for a Photoshopped pop-art image, it's best to choose a shot with good contrast because you'll be, in effect, using the shadows as a black outline for your colours. Without good shadow detail to define the face, your subject may look like they're without a nose or mouth. If you're unsure, check the image by turning it black & white and then clicking *Image>Adjustment>Threshold* to play with the slider to see if enough detail is retained. You should also try to pick an image with a background that contrasts with the subject to make it easier to extract with the Magic Wand Tool. Some shots work better than others, but it's a case of trial and error. So what are you waiting for, give your shots a new lease of life with this graphic Photoshop technique.

Get ready!

TIME REQUIRED
15 MINUTES

EQUIPMENT NEEDED
ADOBE PHOTOSHOP CS4

Be a wand wizard!

If you struggle selecting the whole background, increase or decrease the Tolerance level of your wand slightly and hold *Shift* while making multiple selections.

1 Open the image and drag the Background Layer onto the new layer icon to duplicate the layer. Now add a new coloured layer between the two layers by clicking *Layer> New Layer*, then *Edit>Fill Layer* and pick a colour. Drag this layer between the two and click the top layer.

2 Use the Magic Wand Tool to select the background and hit delete to show the coloured background behind. Go to *Select> Deselect*, then *Image> Adjustments> Desaturate* and *Image> Adjustments> Threshold*, adjusting the slider to retain facial details.

3 Add a touch of blur by going to *Filter>Blur> Gaussian Blur* and setting the slider to 1px. Drag the top layer onto the New Layer icon to duplicate. Select the Paint Bucket Tool and hit *X* to select a white foreground and click the face. (*X* changes the foreground colour from black to white).

4 Select the top layer's blending mode to Multiply. Click the second layer and create a Solid adjustment layer (the split circle icon on the Layers palette). Choose a colour to use as a skin tone, then select the Paint Bucket Tool, hit *X*, and fill the layer with black to mask the colour.

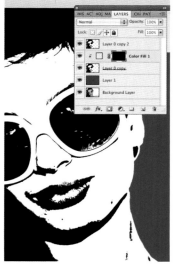

5 Hold *Alt* and click between the second and third layer. Now select the Brush Tool and hit *X* to choose a white foreground colour and paint over the skin area. Create another Solid colour adjustment layer, choose a second colour, clip the layer below and repeat for each colour.

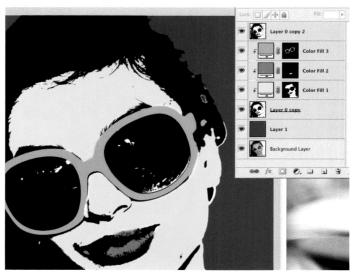

6 Select the Crop Tool and hold down *Shift* while dragging from top left to bottom right to create a square image. Move the square until you're happy with the crop. Double click to complete. Select all layers except the Background Layer by holding Shift and clicking on each layer.

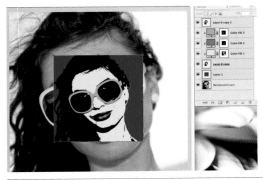

7 Hit *Cmd+T* to enter Free Transform. In the options at the top, change the percentages to 50% for width and height, and move the image to the top left of the picture. Select the Move Tool, hold *Alt*, drag the shot to the top right, making a copy of the image. Repeat three times and position the boxes on the page.

8 To change the background colours, scroll down the Layers palette to select the right layer, then choose a colour and use the Paint Bucket Tool on the square. For other features you want to change the colour of, double click on the corresponding layer's coloured box to bring up the colour picker.

I spy with my little eye...

MATTY GRAHAM: If you flick through the pages of your favourite magazines and take a minute to look at the different portraits splashed across the pages, one thing should become fairly clear. On the whole, it's the funny, edgy and quirky portraits that grab your attention more than the serious, dull and mundane shots. The theory can be extended to your photographic portraiture work, whether you're shooting a campaign ad, or you just want to take some quirky shots of the kids.

As parents know, children have the attention span of a goldfish, and the more energy and fun you can bring to the photoshoot, the longer the child is likely to give you their attention, resulting in ultimately better portraits.

To test this theory, we invited seven-year-old Alfie to have his portrait taken. We weren't aiming to shoot the standard 'head and shoulders' shot however. With the help of one simple prop – a magnifying glass – our aim was to create a simple yet quirky result that you can try at home too.

1 My first job is to prepare for Alfie's arrival. The less time I spend adjusting the set-up for when my subject arrives, the more time I'll have to take photos before he becomes tired or bored. I want to use a coloured background, so I tape some coloured paper to the back of some rigid cardboard and position it in place by a wall.

2 I need to light my subject, but also throw some light towards the background to create an interesting vignette. I position one studioflash fitted with an Rotalux softbox to the right of the camera at a 45° angle and then place a second studioflash as close to the background as possible. Both units are set to half power.

3 To make sure I have the right exposure settings before Alfie arrives, I put the camera on self-timer mode and take some test shots using myself as a stand-in model. I set my camera to manual mode and dial in a shutter speed of 1/160sec (ISO 100). It's then a case of trying different apertures – in the end I settle on f/13.

Make photoshoots fun

Kids like nothing more than messing around and pulling faces. Try to harness this energy and use it in your portfolios. Ask kids to pull their scariest face and let them change clothes to bring variety to the shoot.

4 When Alfie arrives, I place him in position and spend some time texplaining the shots we're trying to capture. We also run through lots of expressions he should pull to make the images more fun.

5 My aim is to capture the image in-camera, but after a few test shots it's obvious that this may not be the best approach. As you can see, the magnifying glass distorts Alfie's eye and doesn't look natural.

 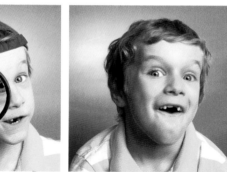

6 Some simple post-processing work will be necessary to correctly produce the magnified eye, but first I need to take the best possible portrait. I swap the blue background to red to contrast better with Alfie's shirt. I shoot two types of portrait – one of Alfie holding the magnifying glass and one of him without it but with a similar expression. With the second shot, it's essential to get the eye as sharp as possible as it will soon be enlarged.

7 I use the Elliptical Marquee Tool to draw a circle around his unobscured eye and copy and paste it to the image with the magnifying glass. I drag the Guide lines to create a frame around the area of glass. I then use the Elliptical Marquee Tool again to draw my circle, which is limited to the size created by the Guide lines. I click *Select>Modify>Feather* and enter 1 pixel.

8 I then select *Layer>New Layer* and then *Edit>Paste Into*, which pastes the area of Alfie's eye from my previous 'expression shot' into my circle selection. The eye is still the original size so to make it look magnified, I click *Edit>Free Transform* and then (holding shift to keep the dimensions the same) drag the corners out to increase the size of the eye.

9 To really give a natural magnified look to the eye, I click *Filter>Distort>Pinch* and drag the slider amount to -29 – feel free to experiment to see what works best with your image. Once I'm happy with the position of the eye (which can be adjusted with the Move Tool) and it's centred in the middle of the glass, I flatten the layers and save my file as a TIFF.

Final image
I spy a fun portrait that's
not only fresh and vibrant
but also looks like it was
shot in-camera.

Black & white in portraits

There are several factors that you need to consider when you shoot images that you plan to convert to monochrome

THE STRENGTH OF a monochromatic picture is determined by its raw components: form, composition and tonal range all have to be at their strongest. As well as geometry, there has to be a good balance of tones throughout the picture so that the eye is not forced to linger on areas that are too black or white heavy and encourage it to move around the whole image. It's amazing how many brilliant colour images fail when they are turned into monochrome and how many images that don't work in colour can come to life as a black & white conversion!

The whole concept of black & white is so different to colour that you have to pre-visualise the scene, and this isn't an easy thing to do. For example, if you have a subject wearing a blue coat and they stand against green foliage, the tones will end up being very similar in black & white due to the limited tonal separation, and thus you'll lose the depth between foreground and background. In a colour image, you can see the depth because of the disparity between the green and blue, but in mono that same image will look flat and two-dimensional. It's the distinction between the relative lightness and darkness of tones that becomes so important in monochrome pictures. You have to think about tonality that much more. There is a monochromatic filter on the market that can help. You put it to your eye and hold it up to a scene and, while it doesn't remove the colour in its entirety, it does reduce it somewhat. It's a definite aid for evaluating a scene's monochromatic potential in terms of tonal range and geometry.

To capture your best black & white pictures, you need to get used to thinking in a colourless world and pick your model and background appropriately. For example, if your location has green foliage you would be better off choosing a model with blonde rather than brown hair. Blonde hair will look that much lighter in monochrome and provide better separation from this sort of background. If you have to work with a specific model, you might think about moving them across to a different background if things don't look tonally distinct, or perhaps change their clothes if background choice is limited.

Mono magic
While this colour image is striking, as a black & white, its composition and tonal range has made it even more dynamic and visually pleasing.

Black & white plug-ins

SILVER EFEX PRO 2 €199.95 (around £175)
Nik Software / www.niksoftware.com

Fully-featured plug-in for Photoshop, Elements, Lightroom and Aperture that delivers top-quality conversions. The interface borrows much from the traditional darkroom, including the ability to simulate black & white films and manipulate parts of the picture selectively with Control Points. Expensive but very powerful.

BLACK & WHITE STUDIO €30 (around £26)
Power Retouche / www.powerretouche.com

Affordable and full of features, Black & White Studio offers a large number of adjustable parameters, including colour sensitivity. Exposure as well as highlight and shadow detail can be controlled individually, and 'print quality' can be adjusted to emulate different contrast grades of photographic paper.

BW WORKFLOW PRO $19.90 (around £12)
Fred Miranda / www.fredmiranda.com

The principal behind this plug-in is control – and lots of it. You can take charge over literally every aspect of mono conversion with BW Workflow Pro, from coloured filters to duotone and tritone presets. Even dynamic range is handled with ease, and the plug-in can simulate black & white infrared photography too.

BJORN THOMASSEN

THE TOP TEN WAYS OF CONVERTING TO MONOCHROME

There is more than one way to convert a photograph to black & white. Some are easy, others more involved. Some allow no control at all, others give more than you could ever want. Here are ten Photoshop techniques to get you started – if you know of any more, please do let us know!

1) *Grayscale mode* Switching from RGB to Grayscale mode (***Image>Mode>Grayscale***) dumps all colour information.

2) *Desaturate* In the ***Image> Adjustments*** menu, select Desaturate to drain the colour from your image in one click.

3) *Convert to B&W* The Black & White command, found in the ***Image>Adjustments*** menu is a more controllable way to turn to mono. You can add it as an adjustment layer too.

4) *Channel Mixer* Choose ***Image>Adjustments>Channel Mixer***. Tick the monochrome box and now you can play with colour sensitivities with the red, green and blue sliders.

5) *Just one channel* Looking at just one channel will give you a black & white view. Choose the one that gives the best result from the Channels palette (***Windows>Channels***)

6) *Gradient Map* Often discovered by mistake as it's the next command down from Channel Mixer in the ***Image> Adjustments*** menu, the Gradient Map can be used to send an image to pure black & white

7) *Hue/Saturation* A Hue/ Saturation adjustment layer with the saturation slider moved all the way down to the left will remove colour from your image. And it's non-destructive too.

8) *LAB Colour* In LAB colour mode (***Image>Mode>LAB***) choose either A or B from the Channels palette. Both will give you a mono result.

9) *Raw files* The latest version of Adobe Camera Raw works with monochrome images. Click the HSL tab and you'll be presented with colour sensitivity sliders so you can mimic the effect of using coloured optical filters.

10) *Duotone* Not strictly mono, but we wanted to include it here anyway. Duotone images use black, white and an extra colour for a subtle tint. With a Grayscale image choose ***Image>Mode> Duotone*** and experiment or try one of the built-in presets.

Create a film noir portrait

Adding grain to monochrome portraits can give them a timeless film feel. Find out how to shoot a gritty and nostalgic low-key portrait

THERE ARE VERY FEW instances when we'd ask you to try and light a portrait for deep shadows and high contrast, but it seems to suit low-key monochrome, adding drama and mystery. We'd also normally advise you to steer clear of digital noise because its grain can ruin a shot, but when trying to simulate an old black & white film photograph, there's nothing quite like a bit of grain to add authenticity.

As opposed to a high-key portrait that's very clean and bright with light tones, a low-key portrait is gritty and moody with predominantly dark tones. It's actually quite easy to accomplish, as you only need one light and don't have to be overly concerned with unflattering shadows. You don't need studioflash either, you can use window light instead, but you should use a black background to enhance the dark tone of the picture. If you position your subject next to a window, remember to use a net curtain to soften the light and as you'll probably use aperture-priority mode, you may want to bracket

the exposures or add a couple of stops of negative exposure compensation. You'll probably find that the camera's metering can be easily tricked and the best image is the one that's underexposed. You want to end up with a shot that has the lit elements exposed while the rest of the image is in the dark.

For this step-by-step, we've used a single Elinchrom D-Lite 4IT head with a softbox. While you could set your camera to a high ISO to increase digital noise, you'd be better to apply grain using Photoshop to record a sharper result. To add to the 1920's film effect, we asked our subject to wear a hat for added texture and interest and to wear dark clothes so that the attention is drawn to her face and the lighting sharply falls off into blackness.

As well as adding noise in Photoshop, there are also a lot of plug-in filters available, including the brilliant Silver Efex package by Nik Software that offer you a greater level of control and creativity over your film noir image.

1 Position the subject a few metres from the backdrop so that none of the light from the softbox falls on it, turning it grey or highlighting wrinkles and creases.
If using flash, switch your camera to manual mode and set the shutter speed to 1/250sec (or whatever your camera's flash sync speed is) and the ISO to its lowest rating. You'll need to adjust the aperture to control how the subject is exposed.

2 Position the studioflash head slightly in front of and at a similar height to the subject, approximately a metre away, and set to its lowest power. Take a test shot at f/5.6 to see how well the face is exposed and then close the aperture (ie underexpose) until most of the shot is dark, with only the part of the face you're trying to light well exposed. We found between f/10 and f/13 worked well.

Wrong Right

3 Varying the light's distance from the subject as well as the aperture will limit the light that reaches the face and can help achieve a better effect. Be watchful of where the light falls on the subject though – the eyes are important in a portrait, so make sure these are well exposed by altering the angle or height of the light or turning the subject slightly more towards it.

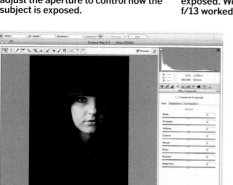

4 Open your favourite image in Adobe Camera Raw and make whatever adjustments you feel you need to under the Basic tab, then switch to the HSL/Grayscale tab and click on Convert to Grayscale to convert the image to mono. You can then adjust the colour sliders to tweak the tones. In this case the Orange slider improved the skin tone.

5 Once you're happy with your picture, click OK to open it in Photoshop. Apply any cropping that you require and then duplicate the layer (Layer> Duplicate Layer) and work on it using the Healing Brush Tool (see last issue's Photoshop for Photographers for details) to get rid of any blemishes. You're now ready to add the grain.

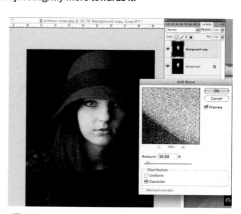

6 With the duplicate layer selected, go to Filter>Noise>Add Noise to open the Add Noise dialogue box. The Gaussian distribution will have a much stronger effect than Uniform but places random noise across the image, which is closer in effect to what film would do. Adjust the Amount slider until you're happy with the level of noise.

Final image
As the noise will be added to the shadows, you'll probably find that the blacks turn slightly grey. To correct this, go to *Layer> New Adjustment Layer>Brightness/Contrast* and then adjust the Contrast slider slightly.

Add a touch of tone

Bring mood to mono by toning images with a tint of colour. Here are just a few ways of adding colour using Photoshop

ADDING APPROPRIATE TONES to a black & white image can imbue pictures with subtle moods. Photoshop offers many variations in colour and more control over toning than traditional chemical treatments. Adding a monochromatic (single) colour can not only make an image more aesthetically pleasing but alter the feel too. Blue will give an image a cool finish and is ideally suited to wintery scenes, while sepia provides warmth and an effect reminiscent of photos from yesteryear. For more complicated toning, and to combine an extensive colour palette, Photoshop also offers duotone, tritone and quadtone effects that allows a photographer to blend two or more colours.

Method One: **Hue/Saturation**

This is a fairly straightforward way of adding colour. Open the Hue/Saturation dialogue box (**Image>Adjustments>Hue/Saturation**). The quickest way is **Cmd/Cntrl + U**. The first thing to do is tick the Colorize and Preview boxes. Now alter the Hue slider, which creates a range of colours to choose from. You can alter the intensity of the colour by increasing or decreasing the Saturation slider. Leave the Lightness slider alone. You can Colorize a colour photo but the results are not as smooth as converting to Grayscale and back to RGB.

Hue/Saturation is a very simple process to try and a great introduction to toning for beginners.

Method Two: **Photo Filter**

Another easy way to alter the colour is using **Image>Adjustments>Photo Filter**, which is available in Adobe Elements and Photoshop CS. Again convert to grayscale then back to RGB. This is a group of colours that mimic certain camera filters. Choose a colour from the Filter drop-down menu or click the Colour box to bring up the Colour Picker where you can create your very own colour. Tick Preserve Luminosity or the image will go rather flat and lifeless. The Density slider allows you to create a subtle or heavy colour effect.

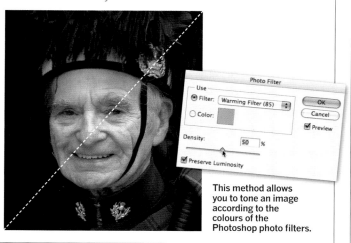

This method allows you to tone an image according to the colours of the Photoshop photo filters.

Method Three: **Duotones**

Traditionally, many monochrome images have been printed reprographically (CMYK) as duotones using two or more colours to 'beef up' the contrast and tonal range. Normally you would choose black for the shadows and one other colour, usually grey, for mid-tones and highlights. But for a more dramatic toning effect, try substituting the grey for a colour or add several colours to the mix.

This toning process gives photographers the option of adding extra colours to their image, making tritone (three colours) or even quadtone (four colours) pictures. Keeping it simple though usually gives the best results. While this is the most involved of the four techniques covered here, it is relatively straightforward and we'd recommend you give it a try to see for yourself how easy it is to create some nice effects.

First of all change the image to Grayscale (**Image>Mode>Grayscale**) followed by **Image>Mode>Duotone**. A dialogue box opens with black as the default Ink 1. Select the Type drop-down menu to select Duo/Tri/Quadtone. Double-click the white box in Ink 2 and the Custom Colors box appears. Choose a general colour by using the colour slider and click a specific colour from the boxes on the left. You can double-click the Curves dialogue box on the right of Ink 1 to alter the contrast and brightness of each colour. This technique works well when printed on inkjet printers, which also use CMYK inks.

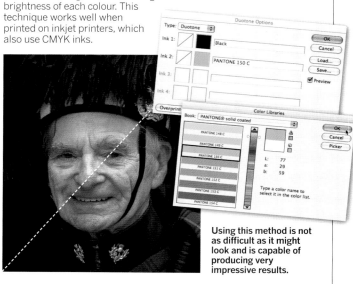

Using this method is not as difficult as it might look and is capable of producing very impressive results.

Method Four: **Gradient Map**

This technique is perhaps a little gimmicky but if you like 1970's psychedelic effects, then you might want to give it a try! Go to **Image>Adjust>Gradient Map** and click on the graduated box (not the arrow) to reveal the dialogue box. Click on a colour and use the sliders to play around with the effect. It gives a dramatic pseudo-solarised effect, which may occasionally be useful. You can explore this tool further by creating your own colour gradients, choose colours similar to duotones for a split-toned effect.

We've selected a subtle black to brown gradient but you can create your own and create unusual effects.

Final Image
To create this toned image we used the duotone technique and selected Pantone 105 as the second colour.

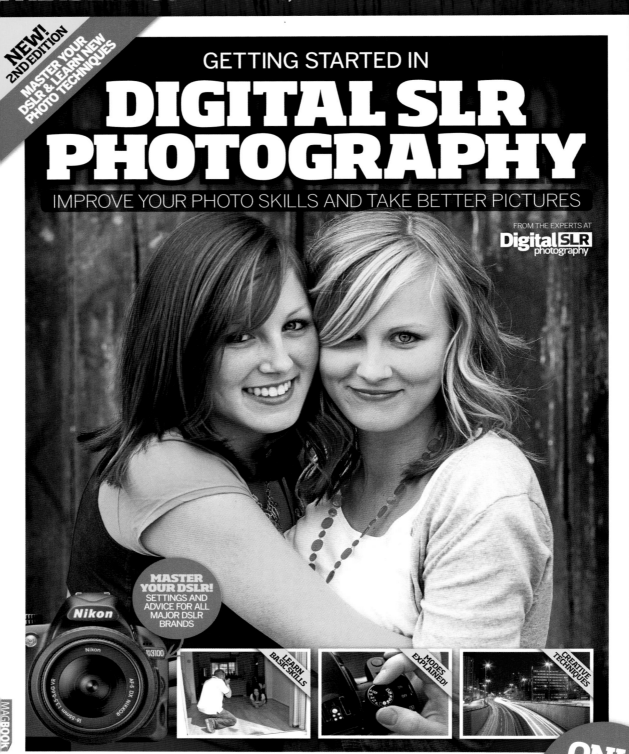

PORTRAIT GEAR

EXPERT ADVICE TO HELP YOU CHOOSE AND USE THE BEST KIT FOR SHOOTING PORTRAITS

The best lenses for portraits

The standard kit zoom supplied with your DSLR is a good general purpose lens that is suitable for taking portraits, but we'd recommend you consider one of these two types of optics for better quality results

The 'standard' 50mm f/1.8

In the days of 35mm film SLRs, you'd invariably find a 50mm f/1.8 prime lens attached to the front of virtually every SLR. It was the first lens that virtually everyone with an SLR used and remained popular until the late eighties. It was around this time that standard zooms started to appear. With variable focal lengths ranging from wide-angle to short-telephoto, the 28-70mm (and similar) lens represented a step forward in terms of flexibility and sadly it led to the demise of the 50mm as the standard lens of choice. However, its popularity has recently seen a resurgence for a number of reasons.

The first is that it's a very inexpensive lens to get hold of. With 50mm lenses from the likes of Canon, Nikon and Sony costing just over £100 new, and used versions available for a little over half that, they're an affordable choice for most of us. To add further credence to the value-for-money argument, consider this fact. The lens of choice for many portrait pros has long been the 85mm telephoto, which for an f/1.8 version will set you back around £300. If your DSLR uses an APS-C sensor, as most do, a 50mm that costs you £100 equates to a 75mm f/1.8 (or 80mm f/1.8 if you use Canon) – but with an effective saving of around £200!

Also, if you don't mind buying a used manual focus lens, you can pick one up for around £25. So for the price of a decent memory card, you can get a high-quality piece of glass that may be a few decades old and lack AF, but won't leave you wanting in the optical department. So, there's no denying a 50mm lens is affordable,

but what else does it offer? Well, the biggest selling point must surely be its maximum aperture of f/1.8. Having a lens with such a fast maximum aperture offers stacks of potential. With your average 18-55mm having a maximum aperture of f/3.5-5.6, the 50mm is two to three stops faster, giving a brighter viewfinder image and allowing you to shoot handheld in low light, while using lower ISO ratings than you would normally get away with.

The main benefit of the wide maximum aperture is the extremely shallow depth-of-field when you shoot wide open, which helps isolate the main subject from its surroundings. This single feature provides significant creative opportunities, especially in the field of portraiture. The 50mm also scores better than virtually any lens in the size and weight department. Weighing around 150 grams and measuring about 5cm in length, it's the perfect optic to keep with you, especially when you're travelling and storage is at a premium.

The final benefit is possibly the most important – image quality. As with the majority of prime lenses, the optical quality from the humble 50mm lens is arguably better than all but the high-end zooms and in terms of sharpness, is far superior to a standard zoom. In terms of sharpness, distortion, light fall-off and contrast and even when used wide open, you'll have little to complain about. So, there you have it, a small, lightweight and highly affordable lens with a super-fast aperture and razor-sharp optics. Is it not time you bought one?

What's the big deal about the 50mm's f/1.8 aperture?

You have to experience a lens as fast as the 50mm to really understand and appreciate its benefits but, trust us, once you've tried you'll be hooked. The 50mm's f/1.8 aperture enables you to throw the background completely out of focus and isolate the main subject from its setting. This set of images shows the changes in depth-of-field at various apertures from f/1.8 to f/22.

f/1.8

f/3.2

f/5.6

f/8

f/11

f/14

f/18

f/22

Telephoto zooms

IN THE LATTER YEARS of the film era, the 70-300mm was the most popular choice of telezoom due to the versatility of its focal lengths. For most digital SLR users, the 55-200mm covers a similar zoom range, thanks to the 1.5x effective increase in focal length associated with the smaller sensor size. That's great news, as a 55-200mm lens is smaller and lighter than a 70-300mm lens and its also far more affordable.

The 55-200mm zoom is suitable for a wide variety of subjects. At its widest end, it's perfect for general portraiture, while zooming to the telephoto end is ideal if your subject is further away or you are shooting candids. There is a wide number of 55-200mm zooms available and all produce a decent performance, although we've featured the Nikon and Tamron zooms as they offer particularly good value for money. Most 55-200mm lenses are budget zooms, offering good enough quality for general purpose photography, but if you're intending to produce large prints, you should look at upgrading to a mid-range zoom with a faster maximum aperture and better optics. We've included Canon's 70-200mm f/4L USM as its one of the best in its class. You may find stores try selling you a 70-300mm, which effectively behaves as a 105-450mm. While a great choice for digital SLRs with a full-frame sensor, we'd not recommend the 70-300mm for use with cameras using the APS-C sensor due to problems associated with the increased focal length, such as camera shake and its restrictive angle-of-view at close range.

Canon EF 70-200mm f/4L USM

Guide Price: £790
Street Price: £550
www.canon.co.uk

Lens optics:	16 elements in 13 groups
Lens mount:	Metal
Maximum aperture:	f/4
Minimum aperture:	f/32
Minimum focus:	1.2m
Filter thread:	67mm
Weight:	705g
Supplied accessories:	None
Dimensions:	76x172mm
Compatibility:	All Canon EOS models

Canon has a number of budget zooms and also a couple of pro-spec f/2.8 options. This is one of two mid-range f/4 lenses (the other offers an image stabiliser) and arguably the best value of Canon's four 70-200mm zooms. It boasts an f/4 maximum aperture throughout its range and these faster optics result in it being a longer and heavier zoom than budget alternatives. However, this drawback is soon forgotten once you use it – the autofocus is whisper-quiet and very accurate, while the image quality is far superior to cheaper zooms, with less distortion, far more detail and better contrast. Unless you're a pro requiring the f/2.8 maximum aperture, this lens (or the more expensive IS version) is good enough for all your needs. Well worth checking out.

Verdict

It costs far more than budget zooms but optical quality is far superior and worth the extra.

Handling	★★★★★
Features	★★★★★
Autofocus	★★★★★
Image quality	★★★★★
Value for money	★★★★☆

OVERALL	★★★★★

Nikon AF-S VR DX 55-200mm f/4-5.6G ED

Guide Price: £320
Street Price: £210
www.nikon.co.uk

Lens Optics:	15 elements in 11 groups
Lens mount:	Plastic
Maximum aperture:	f/4-5.6
Minimum aperture:	f/22-32
Minimum focus:	1.1m
Filter thread:	52mm
Weight:	335g
Supplied accessories:	Case and hood
Dimensions:	73x99.5mm
Compatibility:	APS-C Nikon & Fujifilm models

This version sits alongside the original Nikon DX 55-200mm G ED Nikkor lens but boasts a VR (Vibration Reduction) facility. The result is a slight increase in the size and weight but more importantly improved performance in low light and at the telephoto end due to shake being minimised. The Nikon boasts a very wide zoom ring but the slim manual focus ring at the end of the barrel could do with more width. The autofocus is quick, quiet and responsive even in low light and is one of the better lenses in terms of sharpness. As with other zooms of this type, images at the wide to mid-focal lengths are better than at 200mm. At maximum aperture sharpness is fair, and improves significantly as soon as the lens is stopped down, proving best at f/8-13.

Verdict

A great telezoom thanks to decent all-round performance and the VR facility.

Handling	★★★★☆
Features	★★★★☆
Autofocus	★★★★☆
Image quality	★★★★☆
Value for money	★★★★☆

OVERALL	★★★★☆

Tamron AF 55-200mm f/4-5.6 LD Di II

Guide Price: £160
Street Price: £120
www.intro2020.co.uk

Lens Optics:	13 elements in nine groups
Lens mount:	Plastic
Maximum aperture:	f/4-5.6
Minimum aperture:	f/32
Minimum focus:	0.95m
Filter thread:	52mm
Weight:	300g
Supplied accessories:	Hood
Dimensions:	71.6x83mm
Compatibility:	APS-C (various fittings)

This zoom has proven extremely popular thanks to a combination of low price, decent build quality and good all-round performance. The wide zoom ring is very easy to grip and has a nice action, but as with the Nikon, the manual focusing ring is thin and not the easiest to use. The autofocus turns in a good performance – it's not the quickest or quietest but it is accurate and performs better than expected in low light. As with most 55-200mm zooms, it performs best at the shorter end but quality through the range is good, especially once the aperture is stopped down, with f/8-11 giving the sharpest results. Please note this lens is designed for use with APS-C sensors only and isn't compatible with larger sensor sizes. It is available in Canon, Nikon and Sony fittings.

Verdict

A budget zoom lens that turns in a better performance than you expect for the price.

Handling	★★★★☆
Features	★★★★☆
Autofocus	★★★☆☆
Image quality	★★★★☆
Value for money	★★★★☆

OVERALL	★★★★☆

Studioflash for enthusiasts

If you're serious about studioflash, you need a kit to match your passion. A more advanced set of lights will meet your needs for extra features, power and performance, giving you the tools to get better results. These three outfits from leading brands offer excellent value, a great range of features and first-class performance

Elinchrom D-Lite 4 IT Studio 2 Go kit

Guide Price: £669
Street Price: £549*
www.theflashcentre.com
Sophisticated budget studioflash

Elinchrom are one of the top brands in studioflash and have long been recognised for delivering high quality, reliable products. However, in the past, the prices of the Swiss firm's outfits meant they were usually reserved for enthusiasts and professionals. That changed with the launch of its D-Lite system in 2006, a budget kit that brought the quality of Elinchrom to the masses. It has proved to be a best-seller and four years on, Elinchrom hope its updated outfits enjoy similar success.

These new models aren't just a simple redesign and the odd feature addition either, they offer real improvements over the original set, which itself was excellent. The 'IT' in the name stands for Intelligent Triggering and hints at the biggest changes to the heads. The inclusion of an intelligent, programmable slave cell enables it to synchronise with 'strobist' Speedlite systems (in other words the heads won't fire due a flashgun's pre-flash). Also, and in our view more importantly, there's a built-in Skyport receiver. This allows the heads to be triggered wirelessly, (in other words without the need of a sync lead) using a hotshoe-mounted Skyport Eco transmitter, which is supplied as part of the kit. The Skyport system is a radio trigger with four frequencies (just on the off-chance someone nearby has one, you can set a different frequency so you don't keep setting each other's lights off! It allows for fast flash syncs up to 1/250sec, as well as a standard setting of 1/160sec).

The heads are available in 200 and 400-Watt versions (D-Lite 2 IT & D-Lite 4 IT respectively) and if possible, we recommend you buy the 400-Watt heads as the extra power is very useful.

Elinchrom has taken on board comments from users of its original D-Lite system and have improved its design and construction, with a more robust handle, which houses a spare fuse, and an improved stand fitting that is significantly stronger than its predecessor.

The heads feature a cooling fan that switches on when the internal temperature becomes too high, and has a visual safety indicator should the fan be blocked or stop working. With beginners in mind, it's no surprise to find it's a very easy set of lights to use. Fitting accessories via Elinchrom's tried-and-tested bayonet

The Elinchrom D-Lite IT kits come supplied with everything an enthusiast needs to take their first steps into the world of studio photography.

Shot using the D-Lite 4 IT kit

mount is fast and easy. Should you wish to add to the generous options supplied with the kit, you'll find there is an extensive number of suitable attachments available.

The D-Lite IT's control panel couldn't be easier to use. An LED shows the current power setting with two large buttons beneath allowing it to be increased or decreased. Other controls allow you to set the modelling light to be on at minimum or full power, off, or proportional to the power setting, which is set in 1/10th increments. There is also a button to switch the audible ready 'beep' on or off. Setting up the D-Lite

IT was simple and straightforward to do, taking only a few minutes (preparing the softboxes took the most time). In use, the D-Lite 4 IT worked effortlessly and the Skyport wireless trigger performed perfectly. Recharge times are fast at around one second and the 1/10-stop power adjustments are more than suitable for general studio work.

The D-Lite 4 IT kit has everything you need to get started in studioflash photography and the supplied cases ensure you can easily pack away and protect the kit for storage or for transport from one place to another.

Elinchrom D-Lite kits *

ELINCHROM D-LITE IT 4 STUDIO TO GO TWO HEAD KIT £580
2x D-Lite 4 IT heads;
2x Portalite 66cm softboxes;
1x 16cm reflector;
2x ClipLock stands;
1x Skyport Eco transmitter;
carry cases and cables

ELINCHROM D-LITE IT 2 STUDIO TO GO TWO HEAD KIT £510
2x D-Lite 2 IT heads;
2x Portalite 66cm softboxes;
1x 16cm reflector;
2x ClipLock stands;
1x Skyport Eco transmitter;
carry cases and cables

ELINCHROM D-LITE IT 2/4 TWO HEAD UMBRELLA KIT £475
1x D-Lite 2 IT head;
1x D-Lite 4 IT head;
1x silver umbrella;
1x translucent umbrella; 2x 16cm reflectors; 2x ClipLock stands;
1x Skyport Eco transmitter;
carry cases and cables

All quoted prices are taken from www.theflashcentre.com

Verdict

The Elinchrom D-Lite 4 IT outfit offers a level of reliability, range of features, performance and access to lighting attachments that is hard to match. Whichever outfit you decide to go for, it comes highly recommended.

Build	★★★★☆
Features	★★★★★
Performance	★★★★☆
Value for Money	★★★★★

OVERALL ★★★★★

Elinchrom BXRi 500/500 twin-head kit

Guide Price: £1,020
Street Price: £865
www.theflashcentre.com
Compact studioflash outfit

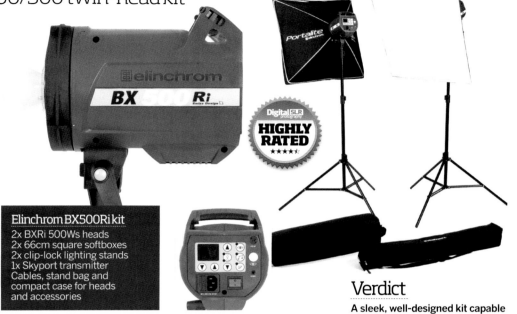

This recent addition to the Elinchrom range combines some of the winning features of its D-Lite budget outfits, with the benefits of the BX range, resulting in a simple but powerful lighting system. The lights come in a choice of 250-Watt and 500-Watt heads, but with a difference in price of just £115 between the twin 250-Watt kit and the twin 500-Watt kit, it's worth opting for the more powerful option.

The lights have a full digital back panel that includes the power display – a five-stop range from 1/16 to full-power – modelling lamp controls, and various flash settings from audible recharge confirmation to pre-flash detection. Multiple button presses can also be used to program additional functions from Intelligent Photo-cell learning mode to EL Skyport controls using the radio trigger system included in the kit. The modelling light can be controlled independently of the flash power, as well as proportionately, via its own set of power buttons.

Like the budget D-Lite kit, the BXRi500 outfit is very compact, and comes in a stylish carry case that looks too small for a full lighting set,

Elinchrom BX500Ri kit

2x BXRi 500Ws heads
2x 66cm square softboxes
2x clip-lock lighting stands
1x Skyport transmitter
Cables, stand bag and compact case for heads and accessories

and a second small stand bag, making the kit very portable. Even when in use, the kit takes up very little room. The heads themselves are stubby and the supplied softboxes are relatively small in size too. The smaller softboxes, however, create a more high-contrast image and require a greater distance for

full-length shots. Results are slightly on the warm side but still very good, and the lights kick out more power than Interfit's Stellar 600. Thanks to the short flash duration, they're also good for freezing motion. The BXRi range competes with the Bowens Gemini, with just £57 between it and the standard Gemini 500R kit.

Verdict

A sleek, well-designed kit capable of delivering a huge amount of power and very advanced control.

Build	★★★★★
Features	★★★★☆
Performance	★★★★★
Value for Money	★★★★☆

OVERALL ★★★★☆

Bowens Gemini 500/500R twin-head kit

Guide Price: £995
Street Price: £900
www.bowens.co.uk
High-quality studioflash system

These are the latest in the Gemini range, and a revamp will see the new Gemini R replacing the Esprit, Esprit DX, Esprit Gemini digital, and Esprit 750 Pro. Bowens' claim that this is 'the world's most advanced monolight' is certainly a bold one, so has it got what it takes? So far there are only 250-Watt and 500-Watt versions but they are both mains and Travel Pak compatible, and feature a twin dial control and a digital display, which shows power information as well as other info from the user set-up mode. These modes include pre-exposure flashes, soft start and lamp-saver options for the modelling bulb, allowing it to dim when left inactive for a set amount of time. The kit includes more sturdy stands than the Gemini 400 kit, and a 60x80cm softbox in addition to a spill kill and silver/white umbrella. An optional remote (RC3) controls functions, and the optional radio trigger is compatible with Pulsar, Litelink and Pocket Wizard devices.

On the side of the head, one dial controls the power in stops, while the second in tenths of stops. On the back panel are the model lamp controls, cell and ready functions,

Elinchrom Gemini kit

2x 500Ws heads
1x Wide reflector
2x 250W modelling bulbs
1x 60x80cm Softbox
1x 90cm Silver/White umbrella
2x Compact lighting stands
1x Sync lead
1x Deluxe trolley case
1x Travel Pak

battery and power inputs. Flash duration is a slower 1/900sec on this model but this is plenty for portrait photography. This kit is also available with the Travel Pak for outdoor use for an extra £300, (more than worth it for the serious snapper). The whole kit fits into a large reinforced case, on a trolley for easy transport. This kit

just oozes quality and professionalism. The results are very natural – slightly warmer than the 400s but not as warm as the Elinchrom BXRi's – and benefit not only from the extra power, but also from the softbox. If you can afford to, opt for the Travel Pak version for added versatility.

Verdict

Stunning outfit that performs brilliantly. Great value, whether or not you choose the Travel Pak.

Build	★★★★★
Features	★★★★★
Performance	★★★★★
Value for Money	★★★★☆

OVERALL ★★★★★

Buyers' Guide: Lighting aids

Whether working with ambient light or shooting in a studio with flash, reflectors and diffusers are an inexpensive and versatile aid to help manipulate light. We show you the main types to consider

THERE IS A COMMON misconception that you need expensive equipment to get professional-looking results. While a better camera and superior optics do make a difference, there are many affordable bits of kit that can lead to far better pictures if used correctly. Lighting aids, in other words reflectors and diffusers, are two such items, proving useful whether you're using daylight, studioflash or virtually any other form of lighting for that matter.

The various technique articles earlier in this guide provide some perfect examples

on how and when to use lighting aids with daylight, but it's worth remembering that they're also suitable for use with any subject that requires lighting control, so are great for still-lifes or close-ups. And of course, they can be used in the studio too: a reflector for instance, is often used to bounce light from the key light source to fill in shadows on the subject, negating the need for a second flash-head.

There are several different types of lighting aids available in different sizes, shapes and colours, from small handheld options to those that require a stand or

assistant to hold them. For the majority of amateurs, a small handheld option is suitable for most needs, while for enthusiast-level upwards, larger reflectors and diffusers prove far more effective, especially when shooting on location.

Our *Buyers' Guide* covers the range of products from all the popular brands that are worth considering for everyday use, but check their websites for more specialist products too. We've also a comparison test of several five-in-one reflector kits, which will help you make the right choice and save you money too.

Reflector size guide

30cm	12in
50cm	20in
56cm	22in
81cm	32in
95cm	37in
107cm	42in
120cm	47in
70x110cm	28x44in
90x120cm	36x48in
100x165cm	40x66in
60x90cm	24x36in
90x125cm	36x50in
100x150cm	39x59in
130x190cm	52x76in
180x245cm	72x98in

California Sunbounce

www.theflashcentre.com

The California Sunbounce range of reflectors is a favourite with professionals thanks to their stability, build quality and light weight. The reflector panels are fitted to aluminium frames that come in various sizes and are quick and easy to assemble, disassemble and pack up for storage and transportation. There is a good choice of reflective panels available, although not every colour is suitable for every frame, but you still have several options open to you (the downloadable PDF catalogue has a very useful easy-reference table).

While you can buy extra panels to use with a frame, the difference in price for complete kits and individual panels isn't that wide, so it's often worth buying the complete outfit to save you having to swap panels while on location. As with other brands, there are silver/white and gold/white reflector options, but you'll find that there are other reflective finishes eg zebra/white (zebra is a mix of gold and silver), as well as a number of translucent diffuser options too.

As they're made for professional use, you'll find that they're relatively expensive, but they are made to last for years of professional use and are produced from the best possible materials. The Sunbounce system is extensive, so

contact importers The Flash Centre if you require further details, or download the catalogue at www.sunbounce.com.

Because the number of options is huge, we've listed the different reflector ranges below and stated the price of the two most popular reflective colours. While a number of sizes are available, we'd recommend the Mini or Pro as your first choice, and the Mega (stated as Big in the catalogue) if you're a very keen enthusiast. Here are the main options:

Micro-mini: (60x90cm)
Silver/white: £101; Zebra/white: £125
Mini: (90x125cm)
Silver/white: £156; Zebra/white: £190
Pro: (130x190cm)
Silver/white: £235; Zebra/white: £275
Big: (180x245cm)
Silver/white: £370; Zebra/white: £430

While a couple of translucent panels are available for the Pro and Mega panels, for diffusing purposes, we'd recommend you check out the Sun Swatter. This is a large diffuser that is ideal for outdoor use as it can be held by a boon over the subject and outside of the image area. It's easy to assemble and designed to be used in windy conditions. There are two sizes available and a number of options for the light-reducing value of the translucent material (1/3, 2/3 or one-stop light diffusion). We'd recommend the smaller Sun Swatter with the 1/3 or 2/3-stop diffuser as a good first option.

Other specialist reflectors in the range includes the Sun-mover, which allows for additional control of the spread of light and the Sun Cage – a purpose made mobile studio for location shooting.

Sun Swatter (130x190cm)
-1/3 stop complete £230
Sun Swatter (130x190cm)
-2/3 Stop complete £240
Sun Swatter Giant (180x245cm)
-1/3 Stop complete £385
Sun Swatter Giant (180x245cm)
-2/3Stop Complete £400

Kenro

www.kenro.co.uk

Kenro produces a circular and a rectangular 5-in-1 kit. The circular reflectors measure 12in, 22in, 32in and 42in and cost £16, £30, £55 and £68 respectively. The rectangular kits measure 28x44in, 36x48in and 40x66in and cost £56, £75 and £99 respectively. All the kits are supplied in a bag with a translucent panel and a reversible gold, silver, white and black cover.

Kenro also offers a range of reflectors and diffusers with handles called Easy

Grips. It has three 60x90cm (24x36in) models in the range, the £41 translucent and the £45 silver/white and sunlight/white variants. Each 5-in-1 reflector kit features a translucent panel over which a reversible gold, silver, white or black cover can be attached. It folds down into a handy round zip bag when not in use.

Calumet

www.calumetphoto.co.uk

Calumet is a major photo retailer and has an extensive number of own-brand photo accessories, including its ZipDisc range of collapsible reflectors. These include two colour reflectors, translucent panels and four-colour sleeves (gold/silver/white/ black) The ZipDisc kits are as follows:

Translucent white ZipDisc panel

The circular diffuser at the heart of its 5-in-1 kit is available on its own too.

56cm £15; **81cm** £26;
107cm £37; **130cm** £46

Zigzag gold-silver/White ZipDisc

The gold-silver side combines gold and silver for added warmth to the subject.

56cm £15; **81cm** £26; **107cm** £37

Silver/white ZipDisc

The classic handheld reflector. Supplied with a zip case.

56cm £15; **81cm** £26; **107cm** £37

ZipDisc Four-colour cover

This four-colour (gold, white, silver and black) sleeve cover can be used on any round or oval reflector.

56cm (22in) ZipDisc reversible: £13
81cm (32in) ZipDisc reversible: £15
107cm (42in) ZipDisc reversible: £16

5-in-1 kit

This is a combination of the ZipDisc translucent panel and the four colour sleeve. We've tested the 81cm 5-in-1 in our comparison test.

56cm £21; **81cm** £34; **107cm** £41

Please note that if you visit Calumet's website, you may get a little confused about the product descriptions, so if you've any queries, phone their customer service on 08706 030303.

Elemental

www.studio-flash.com

Budget studioflash specialists Elemental currently only has two collapsible reflectors in its range, but we've included them in this guide as they represent excellent value for money. Both the 80cm and 107cm 5-in-1 kits comprises a white diffuser with an interchangeable gold, silver and white reflector cover, all supplied in a black bag. The 80cm costs £25, while the 107cm (tested in this issue) is £35. Elemental also has a reflector arm available for £25.

Interfit

www.interfitphotographic.com

Interfit is one of the UK's leading brands of studio equipment and has an extensive range of reflectors, from handhelds to larger stand-supported types, so you've plenty of choice!

■ Soft sun/white; silver/white and silver/gold:

Round, collapsible reflectors available in three finishes and four sizes

30cm £10.50; **56cm** £16.50; **82cm** £27.60; **107cm** £39

■ 5-in-1 kits

These feature a translucent reflector, with a four-colour overlay sleeve (gold, silver, black and white), supplied in a zip-up bag. They are available in three sizes as follows:

56cm £26.50: **82cm** £37; **107cm** £44

■ Easy Grip:

Interfit's Easy Grip reflector has a thick handle for one-handed use and measures 90x60cm (36x24in). It is available in the following colours: sunlight/white; gold/silver; silver/white and ½-stop translucent and costs £40.

■ Portrait Reflector Kit:

Interfit's Portrait Reflector Kit is essentially three reflector panels attached to a frame that fits easily on a lighting stand. Each 90x60cm (36x24in) panel can be individually positioned for improved lighting control. The kit is supplied with one silver/gold panel and two sunlight/silver panels and costs £100.

■ The Large Flat Panel Reflector:

Studio-based photographers may be interested in these large reflector panels, made for full-length portraits and fashion shoots. The Large Flat Panel Reflector measures 89x178cm (35x70in) and is supplied complete with a stand and a rotating/tilting bracket for using the panel vertically or horizontally. Silver/gold and white/black versions are available for £82.

■ Flexi-lite 5-in-1:

This stand-mounted panel reflector is aimed at pros and can be used handheld or on location. The aluminium frame has a boon arm that can be positioned at any angle. Various kits are available in medium (100x150cm) or large (150x200cm). The INT303 has a gold/silver/black/white cover and costs £306.

Lastolite

www.lastolite.com

Lastolite is one of the world's leading studio accessory brands and is particularly renowned for its lighting aids, so it's no surprise to discover it has an extensive range of products. Many are designed for specific pro uses, so due to space constraints, we've selected the products most suitable for general portrait photography. A comprehensive brochure PDF can be downloaded from Lastolite's website if you'd like to check out the entire range.

■ Collapsible reflectors:

When it comes to collapsible reflectors, no brand has as many options as Lastolite. Its round reflectors are available in 30cm, 50cm, 76cm, 95cm and 120cm diameters and there is a huge 1.8x1.2m rectangular option too. All of these are available in the following finishes: silver/white; sunfire/white, silver/gold, sunfire/silver; gold/white and sunlite/soft silver. A two-stop diffuser is also available in all sizes from 50cm upwards. Guide prices for silver/white are as follows: 30cm £13; 50cm £24; 75cm £35; 95cm £58; 120cm £75; 1.8x1.2m £91.

■ Bottletops 5-in-1 kit:

This includes a diffuser panel with elasticated covers. The kit comprises the diffuser panel and a gold/white and sunfire/silver cover and comes in four sizes: 50cm (£41), 75cm (£47), 95cm (£57) and 120cm (£85).

■ TriGrip:

The original TriGrip was the first collapsible reflector to feature a handle and proved extremely popular. The design has been updated, with a new moulded handle improving handling and there are now three sizes in the range: the £47 Mini TriGrip (45cm); £62 TriGrip (75cm) and £77 Large TriGrip (1.2m). For each size, you can choose reflectors in silver/white, gold/white, sunfire/silver and sunlite/softsilver finishes, as well as a one-stop or two-stop diffuser. Accessories for the TriGrip include a support bracket and the TriFlip, a set of seven reflector covers that can be placed over a TriGrip to offer the ultimate in versatility. You can also buy a £185 TriFlip 8:1 kit that supplies a two-stop diffuser (Mini TriGrip or TriGrip) with seven colour sleeves.

■ Triflector:

The MkII kit consists of a support frame with three collapsible panels, all easily packed away in a case weighing a total of only 1.2kg. The panels are available in the following reflective finishes: sunfire/silver, silver/white, gold/white and a 1.2-stop diffuser. A kit is £123; extra sets of panels range from £33-£45.

■ UpLite 4:1:

A set of self-supporting 120x90cm reflector panels for use by photographers working on their own, who need to bounce light at an angle from the floor. The angle can be adjusted from 30-80° and the two panels can be also be separated for handheld use. The UpLite comes in two versions, the Cool Tone has a sunlite/softsilver and silver/white reflective surfaces, while the Warm Tone has a gold/white and sunfire/silver reflective surfaces. It comes supplied with a waterproof shower cap and a carry case and costs £120.

■ Skylite:

Best suited for serious photographers looking for a lightweight, durable and large diffuser that can also double up as a reflector. The rigid, hollow aluminium frame supports a diffuser (0.75 or 1.25 stop) or reflector (gold/silver, silver/white, black/white or sunfire/white) via secure Velcro fastenings. The Skylite can be bought in a number of kit forms and three sizes are available as follows: Small 1.1x1.1m (1.3kg); medium .1x2m (2kg) and large 2x2m (2.3kg). The standard kit includes the frame, silver/white and translucent fabrics and carry bag, and are priced at around £138, £180 and £260 for the small, medium and large respectively.

5-in-1 reflector kits

If you're looking to buy your first lighting aid, make it one of these kits, which offers a silver, white, gold and (rarely used) black finishes. The translucent panel which these reflective sleeves are wrapped around can be used as a very soft white reflector, although its efficiency is poor. You can also use it to shade your subject, although a purpose-made diffuser is obviously far better for this. As we've discovered when conducting this test, in all areas including build quality, all the kits are very similar, so for most photographers, the cheapest option may well be the best one. We've highlighted the major differences below but in truth, they're all very similar products

Elemental 5-in-1 (107cm)

www.studio-flash.com

GUIDE PRICE: £35
STREET PRICE: £35

Better known for their excellent range of budget studioflash, Elemental also offers a couple of 5-in-1 kits that both represent excellent value. This 107cm kit comes in its own black zip-up bag and once removed, the 5-in-1 reflector looks and handles much like the similarly-priced Interfit. The translucent panel is nicely manufactured and the coloured sleeve has a slot for the panel's tab to slip through when zipped up.

The sleeve can be used to give a silver/black or gold/white effect and is thick and well put together. This is a great budget option and excellent value for money.

VERDICT An excellent budget buy.

Build quality (panel)	★★★★★
Build quality (sleeve)	★★★★⯨
Versatility	★★★★☆
Performance	★★★★★
Value for Money	★★★★★
OVERALL	★★★★★

Digital SLR photography **BEST BUY** ★★★★★

Calumet ZipDisc (107cm)

www.calumetphoto.co.uk

GUIDE PRICE: £41
STREET PRICE: £41

Supplied in a zip-up black bag, you'd be forgiven for thinking that once you remove it, this 5-in-1 kit will be identical to the others. In fact it's a little different, with the panel having a thick white rim, as opposed to the black rims found on the others, and a thick, easy-to-hold tab. The sleeve is different too, giving you the choice of gold/silver and white/black finishes, while the metallic colours run right through to the

zips. It's a very well-made kit that should last you years of regular use. As it's an own-brand kit, it is obviously only available directly from Calumet.

VERDICT Nicely made and a good price.

Build quality (panel)	★★★★★
Build quality (sleeve)	★★★★★
Versatility	★★★★☆
Performance	★★★★★
Value for Money	★★★★⯨
OVERALL	★★★★★

Digital SLR photography **BEST BUY** ★★★★★

Kenro 5-in-1 (80cm)

www.kenro.co.uk

GUIDE PRICE: £55
STREET PRICE: £55

The white material of the translucent panel is a little thinner than some but the stitching around the thick black rim is good and overall it's nicely made. The sleeve is near-identical to most others, with thick reflective surfaces, and can be zipped to give silver/black or gold/white options. The panel has a tab but there isn't a slot for it to poke through on the cover. As with the majority of other kits, it is supplied in a

zip-up black bag. While the Kenro proves to be a decent 5-in-1 kit, it is too expensive to compete with rivals, especially as there is no discernible difference in build quality.

VERDICT Good but overpriced.

Build quality (panel)	★★★★☆
Build quality (sleeve)	★★★★★
Versatility	★★★★☆
Performance	★★★★★
Value for Money	★★★☆☆
OVERALL	★★★★☆

Interfit 265 (107cm)

www.interfitphotographic.com

GUIDE PRICE: £44
STREET PRICE: £38

The white surface of the well-made translucent panel offers a ½-stop efficiency and has a thick black edge and small cloth tab for hanging off a hook. The sleeve is made from thick material and can be wrapped around to give silver/black or gold/white options. The zip has a smooth action and at its end, the sleeve has a gap for the tab to stick through. Interfit makes a large number of kits so you should have no

trouble finding the most suitable size for you. Better still, they're available at an excellent price too. A nicely made and high quality kit, supplied in a zip-up black bag.

VERDICT An excellent, affordable kit.

Build quality (panel)	★★★★★
Build quality (sleeve)	★★★★½
Versatility	★★★★☆
Performance	★★★★★
Value for Money	★★★★★
OVERALL	★★★★★

Kenro rectangular (28x44in)

www.kenro.co.uk

GUIDE PRICE: £56
STREET PRICE: £56

As well as its range of circular reflectors, Kenro also has a number of rectangular 5-in-1 kits, with this being the smallest size. Apart from the shape, it's identical to its circular cousin, with a well-made translucent panel and a zip-up sleeve giving silver/black or gold/white options. When shooting full-length portraits, the rectangular shape has the benefit of providing a top-to-toe spread of light when

used vertically. Like the circular kit, the materials used and how it is put together is first-rate, the only question is whether the price will prove inhibitive.

VERDICT Good for full-length portraits.

Build quality (panel)	★★★★☆
Build quality (sleeve)	★★★★★
Versatility	★★★★☆
Performance	★★★★★
Value for Money	★★★½☆
OVERALL	★★★★☆

Lastolite Bottletop 4896 (120cm)

www.lastolite.com

GUIDE PRICE: £85
STREET PRICE: £80

This 120cm kit is the largest in the range, and also the biggest and most expensive 5-in-1 in our test. It's also different in a number of ways. First, the 5-in-1 kit is made up of a panel and two reversible elasticated sleeves: a gold/white and a silver/sunfire. This has a number of benefits: it's quicker to change from one to another as there is no zip, and you can fit one over each side of the panel, allowing you to have different

combinations to suit your liking. The build quality is first-rate, and spare panels are available so you can place a sleeve on each and have two reflectors at the ready.

VERDICT Versatile and made to last.

Build quality (panel)	★★★★★
Build quality (sleeve)	★★★★★
Versatility	★★★★★
Performance	★★★★★
Value for Money	★★★★☆
OVERALL	★★★★★

Overall Verdict

There isn't a great deal of difference between these kits and all should provide many years of use if looked after. The Kenro, Elemental and Interfit kits are very similar but the latter two have price on their side. The Calumet has the slight edge in terms of build quality, but whether this is worth the extra compared to the Interfit and Elemental is debatable. The separate sleeves of the Lastolite allow you to mix and match colours a little and it's extremely well-made, but more expensive. If you're on a budget, we'd recommend the Interfit and Elemental, but for the very best in terms of quality, we'd opt for the Calumet or Lastolite.

General portrait accessories

While not essential, the products covered on these pages will prove extremely useful if you plan to take your portrait photography further. We've selected our favourite accessories, all providing great value for money

Sekonic Flashmate L-308S

Guide Price: £165
Street Price: £150
www.johnsons-photopia.co.uk
Ambient and flash handheld meter

Most photographers are happy with the performance of their camera's metering system, so why would anyone consider splashing out more than a hundred pounds on a handheld meter when it could be spent on a lens, tripod or another useful accessory? Well, in truth, the argument for owning a handheld meter isn't anywhere near as strong as in the days of film, but there are still some valid reasons. For starters, it can be used to measure flash readings (cordless or via a flash sync lead) as well as ambient light, so it's as useful in the studio as it is outdoors. Another benefit is that, by sliding the white dome over the sensor, it can take incident light readings (light falling on the subject), which are more accurate than reflected readings (light bouncing off the subject) – the system used by all

cameras. You can set it to meter in 1/3, 1/2 or full-stop increments, to match how your DSLR works and taking a reading couldn't be easier. Choose the mode (ambient or flash), set the ISO to match your DSLR and then place the meter in front of your subject, facing the camera and press the measuring button. If measuring ambient light, you specify the shutter speed and the meter selects the corresponding aperture. This isn't ideal if you're working in aperture-priority as you need to use the up and down buttons to get to the aperture you want to use and then read off what is the correct shutter speed. The wide LCD on the front has large digits making it easier to read, although there's no backlit function to illuminate it in low light. Out in the field, and in the studio, Sekonic to be extremely accurate and consistent. But with DSLRs offering instant review and histograms, it's no surprise that its appeal is limited. However, if you regularly mix ambient and flash light, you'll find it extremely useful.

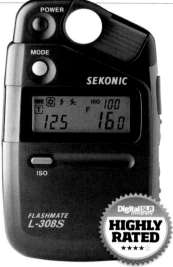

Whether you really need one or not depends on how happy you are with the exposures delivered by your camera and if you plan to regularly shoot flash as well as ambient exposures. If you are considering a light meter, this one is worth a look.

Specifications
Measuring methods: Incident and reflected
Measuring modes: Ambient and flash (corded & cordless)
ISO: 3-8000
Shutter speeds (ambient): 60 seconds to 1/8000sec
Shutter speeds (flash): One second to 1/500sec
Apertures: f/0.5 to f/90.9
EV range: 0 to EV19.9
Power Source: 1x AA battery
Size (WHD): 63x110x22mm
Weight: 95g (including battery)
Supplied accessories: Soft case, strap and Lumidisc

Verdict
Compact, light and a very versatile meter that is the ideal low-cost option for studio and outdoor work.

Build	★★★★☆
Features	★★★★☆
Performance	★★★★☆
Value for Money	★★★★☆

OVERALL ★★★★☆

Nissin Speedlite Di622

Guide Price: £180
Street Price: £100
www.kenro.co.uk
Budget flashgun with lots of features

The Nissin Di622 has excellent build quality for a flash unit that costs around £100, it's as good as models costing twice its price. This flashgun also has some rewarding features that set it apart from many other flashguns at this price range. These include second-curtain sync, slave flash and a standby mode that kicks in after two minutes of non-use to save your battery power. It also includes a flash stand and a diffuser for coverage as wide as 16mm and a fill-in reflector. There is no LCD panel on the rear, instead a series of LEDs indicate power and a single button handles the modes. The Nissin is available for Canon and Nikon DSLRs and considering the features and the reasonable price, offers a decent cut-price option.

Main specifications
Guide Number: 45-62 (ISO 200)
Flash coverage: 16-70mm (24-105mm)
Recycling time: four - six seconds
Bounce facility: Yes (0 to 90º)
Swivel facility: Yes (0 to 270º)
TTL: Yes; **AF assist beam:** Yes
Strobe flash: No; **Wireless:** Yes

Verdict
Well worth the current £100 street price tag. Decent build, features and performance.

Build quality	★★★★☆
Features	★★★☆☆
Performance	★★★☆☆
Value for Money	★★★★☆

OVERALL ★★★★☆

Sigma EF-530 DG Super

Guide Price: £250
Street Price: £200
www.sigma-imaging-uk.com
Highly-sophisticated flashgun

Sigma not only make great value lenses, it also boasts a couple of excellent flashguns, with this being its top model. This model is available in Canon, Nikon, Pentax, Sigma and Sony versions and is packed with stacks of features. In fact, it will take you quite a while to read the EF-530's instruction manual to get to grips with them all! One interesting feature is the High Speed Sync, which allows you to fire the unit at shutter speeds above your camera's usual flash sync speed. The unit can also be used as a master or a slave unit and offers a wide-angle flash diffuser panel. The Sigma is also easy to use with the buttons spaced out and a bright and clear LCD monitor. An excellent flash and well worth considering.

Main specifications
Guide Number: 28-53 (ISO 100)
Flash coverage: 16-70mm (24-105mm)
Recycling time: four - six seconds
Bounce facility: Yes (0-90º)
Swivel facility: Yes (0-270º)
TTL: Yes; **AF assist beam:** Yes
Strobe flash: Yes; **Wireless:** Yes

Verdict
The Sigma offers a decent alternative to more expensive marque flashguns.

Build quality	★★★☆☆
Features	★★★★☆
Performance	★★★★☆
Value for Money	★★★★☆

OVERALL ★★★★☆

Lastolite 1108 background support

Guide Price: £160
Street Price: £150
www.lastolite.com

Portable studio background support

Unless you're working in a custom-built studio, you'll need some form of backdrop for your photography. The most common are either paper rolls or material. The Lastolite background support system is designed to accommodate either of these, and the heavy duty 1150 version can also support the superwhite vinyl backdrops. The kit includes two sturdy lighting stands and a telescopic cross bar to suit different widths of roll or a curtain of up to 3m (1108 model) or 6m (1150 model), the 1150 also uses a third support stand. The system can be constructed in minutes and when not in use, can be easily packed away into a small carry bag. This makes it ideal for those photographers wanting to create a temporary studio set up, or those on the move. However, it is sturdy enough to use on a more permanent basis. Having used this kit in our *Digital SLR*

BEST BUY

Photography studio for several months, we couldn't recommend it enough. Not only is it hard-wearing enough to cope with regular changing of backdrops, and a flurry of models, it comes at a very affordable price too. If you're looking to set up a small studio in your home or garage, then this Lastolite set-up is definitely one to add to your shortlist and represents great value.

Verdict

A simple, affordable solution whether in the studio or home.

Build	★★★★☆
Features	★★★★☆
Performance	★★★★✦
Value for Money	★★★★★

OVERALL ★★★★★

Hama Remote Control 5348

Guide Price: £35
Street Price: £34
www.hama.co.uk

Similar in specification to Nikon's MC-30, the Hama is half the price. It's small, the plastic shell is light at 34g, while its 80cm cord is a good length. The pimpled button has a two-stage action and by sliding it forward it locks into place, with a red strip acting as a visual indicator. It's a no-frills remote that does its job well. It's very affordable compared to marque brands, but faces stiff competition from the Hähnel and Seculine remotes.

Verdict

A reliable, low-cost option.

Build quality	★★★☆☆
Performance	★★★★☆
Value for Money	★★★☆☆

OVERALL ★★★★☆

Hähnel Remote Shutter Release

Guide Price: £25
Street Price: £20
www.hahnel.ie

The Hähnel is larger than the Hama, but this makes it easier to handle, and while its nearly double the weight at around 60g, it's still incredibly lightweight. The two-stage button has a far more positive action and the sliding lock facility is better. The 80cm cord is a useful length but the inclusion of the extension lead is a real bonus. Best of all are the pair of interchangeable connections that allow it to be used with a variety of cameras. A brilliant budget buy.

BEST BUY

Verdict

Perfect choice as a first remote.

Build quality	★★★★☆
Performance	★★★★★
Value for Money	★★★★☆

OVERALL ★★★★★

Seculine Twin-1 R4 Nikon

Guide Price: £50
Street Price: £40
www.intro2020.co.uk

This remote is one of the most versatile models in the budget sector, with both corded and cordless operation to suit your Nikon DSLR. The kit is based around the £35 UT set-up of a wireless transmitter and 50cm cord, but with the addition of a small bulbous receiver that will attach to Nikon DSLRs with the ten-pin socket. If your camera has a built-in infrared receiver, you only need to use the transmitter, if it has the ten-pin socket on the front, such as the D300s, then you can either attach the lead or the receiver. We tested the Seculine with a D300s and found it worked well with both the cord and cordless option. The infrared transmitter proved very effective – at close range it triggered the shutter when used behind or in front of the camera while longer distances required clear line of sight between transmitter and receiver. A small button on the receiver allows it to be set to Bulb, which proved a little fiddly to use, but other than that, it's a well made outfit that's very well priced too. A neat touch is the flashlight mode, which allows you to use the transmitter's small white LED as a torch, useful when shooting in low light! If you use a compatible Nikon DSLR, it's certainly worth checking out.

BEST BUY

Verdict

A versatile remote with lots of features at an attractive price.

Build quality	★★★★★
Performance	★★★★★
Value for Money	★★★★☆

OVERALL ★★★★★

Flash accessories for portraits

There are a wide variety of lighting accessories available for your flashgun, which while not essential for general snaps, can make a difference when you're trying to be more creative with your photography. We highlight a selection of the best diffusers, softboxes and kits for your flashgun

WHILE SOME photographers prefer to only use available light, a true master is able to sculpt light from many sources, with one of the most common being the good old flashgun. Flashes are fantastic for supplementing light so you can get a suitable exposure, but they can also be used to override the ambient light and become more creative with your shots. While a direct, naked flash is sufficient for some situations, many photographers frown on this basic approach to flash photography as the light is rarely flattering and control is limited. So for professional results you need to start looking at adding some complementary accessories to your flash outfit, which will modify the flash to suit your picture and flash effect.

Before picking from the plethora of accessories available, you need to understand the difference between hard and soft light and know the flash effect you want to achieve. In basic terms, hard light produces strong shadows with sharp edges and high contrast, while one that casts weak shadows, with no definite edge, is described as soft light. You also need to decide if want the light to be dispersed and natural-looking or harsher and more selective. The following selection covers every type of accessory that your flashgun could ever need!

Stofen Omni-bounce

Guide Price: £17	Street Price: £11

www.newprouk.co.uk

Some flashguns come supplied with a clip-on diffuser, but if yours doesn't, buy a Stofen. They are devilishly effective in softening the light from your flashgun, with many snappers leaving them attached for all their on-camera flash shooting. They're available for almost every flashgun. Well worth the modest outlay.

OVERALL ★★★★★

Hama Uni Flash Diffuser

Guide Price: £20	Street Price: £16

www.hama.co.uk

A basic flash diffuser that has been made to fit most flashguns on the market. It can be secured to the flashgun with its own Velcro strap, making it suitable for use in the field. The price is a little high but it's worth keeping one in your camera bag, should you have to use a flashgun unit you're not familiar with.

OVERALL ★★★★☆

Lumiquest Softbox III

Guide Price: £45	Street Price: £40

www.newprouk.co.uk

The largest of the Lumiquest range, the Softbox III produces an extremely soft light that is no easy feat when you take the size and portability of it into account. One of the reasons for the great light is that the centre of the front panel is thicker than the edges, which reduces the possibility of a hot spot caused by the head of the flashgun.

OVERALL ★★★★★

Lastolite Ezybox kit (38cm)

Guide Price: £170	Street Price: £160

www.johnsons-photopia.co.uk

While many of the other products have a slight 'DIY' appearance to them, the Ezybox oozes quality and build stability like nothing else in this test. While the Ezybox is value for money for pros, its high price may prove too much for most enthusiasts, even though it offers such a good performance.

OVERALL ★★★★★

Speedlight Pro Beauty Dish

Guide Price: £67	Street Price: £67

www.speedlightprokit.co.uk

When you see the dish in its pre-assembled state, you'd be forgiven for having low expectations. However, once you put it all together things start to look up and then the results blow you away. The value for money is outstanding, as is the quality of the light it produces. One of the best accessories on the market!

OVERALL ★★★★★

Main types of flash accessories

Most flash modifiers fall into one of the following five categories, although some may also overlap

DIFFUSERS:
This is a general term for anything that softens light and is usually in the form of an opaque or white surface, which is placed in front of the flash. Softboxes and standard diffusion domes are the most common type of diffuser.

REFLECTORS:
Bounced light has plenty of opportunity to spread out and, as a result, often softens the light. Reflectors come in white, silver and gold depending on how you want to alter the light's temperature. Beauty dishes also fall into this category.

COLOUR GELS:
These serve one of two purposes – colour correction or colour effects. Colour correction gels are placed over the flash to match the colour of the flash with the temperature of the ambient lighting, such as tungsten or fluorescent. Colour-effect gels change your flash's colour for creative effects.

HONEYCOMB:
Also known as grids, these provide a smoother transition between shadows and highlights than a naked flash. The light falls off more gradually than other modifiers, in a vignette-like manner, which can bring some impressive lighting effects to your images.

SNOOTS:
Designed like a cone, the snoot channels a stream of light that allows you to illuminate certain parts of the scene more selectively for a spotlight effect. They are often used in combination with honeycombs for maximum creative effect.

Honl Flash Kit

Guide Price: £130
Street Price: £110
www.flaghead.co.uk

Contains: Two straps, ¼ Grid, 1/8 Grid, 8in Snoot, 5in Snoot, Gobo bounce card, Colour Correction Kit, Colour Effects Kit

It's not often that a range of products comes along and changes the way that photographers work. But the Honl kit has done just that. The snoots and bounce cards are made from high-grade webbing, which can take the rigours of heavy use. Many of these accessories are available separately but this bundle offers great value for money.

BOUNCE CARD The most obvious use for this card is to use the white side to bounce light off and to soften the light landing on your subject. But it can be used for much more than that. If you get two you then have a simple set of barn doors that allow you to control the spill of the light across your image.

8IN & 5IN SNOOTS The Honl snoots are very versatile pieces of kit, which lend themselves to a number of applications. They can be used closed to direct the light from your flashgun in a very direct, almost spotlit manner, so you can highlight one element in your camera's viewfinder. Alternatively, you can open the snoot, which works in the same manner as a bounce, directing the light up and forward towards your subject.

¼ GRID & 1/8 GRID SPOTS These grids look and feel very robust and attach to your flashgun by combining with the Speed Strap (included in the kit). Once attached the strong Velcro holds incredibly well so you'll have no worries about the grids slipping.

COLOUR CORRECTION GEL & COLOUR EFFECTS KIT Possibly the highlight of the Honl kit, these easy to use gels are fast becoming one of the most popular accessories for flasht. Using the Speed Strap, the gels have Velcro edges and attaching them to the flashgun is easy and hassle-free as you just place the gel over the flash and push on the Velcro until it takes hold. Just like the Honl grids, the gels stay in place securely and cover the whole flashgun.

Verdict

The price isn't low but the quality of the kit is superb. The outfit slips easily into just about any camera bag, weighs next to nothing and is really simple to set up.

Build quality	★★★★★
Features	★★★★★
Performance	★★★★★
Value for money	★★★★☆

OVERALL ★★★★★

Interfit Strobies Portrait Flash Kit

Guide Price: £120
Street Price: £100
www.interfitphotographic.com

Contains: Flashgun Mount, Globe, Beauty dish, Softbox, Barn Doors, Snoot and Honeycomb

The Interfit Strobies kit is a scaled down version of larger studio accessories, so while the attachments are fairly sturdy, they aren't very compact or easy to transport, particularly the Globe option that is shaped like a small football. The accessories attach to a mount before they fit to a flashgun, so you'll need a separate mount if you wish to use more than one flashgun at a same time, which is highly likely.

SOFTBOX The softbox is a miniature version of the one you get in studios and is also just as difficult to assemble. We would only recommend this softbox for a home studio as you wouldn't want to put it together more than once. That said, once assembled, the build quality is decent and as long as it isn't given too much abuse, it should give you a good few years of service.

BEAUTY DISH The small beauty dish can be slipped on to the kit's standard mount and, despite its compact size, delivers an even spread of light. Unlike some models, when attached, this lightweight dish won't make your flashgun feel top-heavy.

GLOBE DIFFUSER This is an unusual piece of equipment that attaches to your flashgun via a supplied mount. For the best results, you will have to set your flashgun head to bounce (so it's pointing towards the ceiling) before attaching the diffuser. Once triggered, the dome fills with light and then emits the light in a spherical direction. Be careful when attaching the Globe, as one fall on to a hard surface will most likely crack it into pieces.

BARNDOOR The barndoor has four flaps that allow you to 'cover up' some of the light from your flashgun for more control over its distribution. When using the barndoors open, the light from the flashgun spreads over a wide area and makes an ideal accessory for a background light. The build quality is okay, but don't match the Honl kit.

SNOOT & HONEYCOMB The Snoot and Honeycomb work in combination with each other. With the Snoot fixing to the mount, it can be used on its own to create a spotlight. The Honeycomb grid slides down the barrel of the Snoot and is dense enough to block the light quite well.

Verdict

This kit has some useful applications and would prove a frugal and rewarding buy for the photographers taking their first steps with flashgun accessories.

Build quality	★★★★☆
Features	★★★★☆
Performance	★★★★☆
Value for money	★★★★☆

OVERALL ★★★★☆

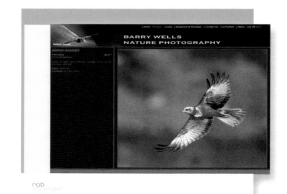

Be sure to bracket!
Whether you use the grey card or not, in tricky lighting conditions, bracket your exposure by +/-1 stops using your camera's exposure compensation or AEB functions to ensure you get the shot

Metered to perfection!
Scenes with strong backlighting can lead to exposure error. Use a grey card and you should have no problems.

How to use your free metering & White Balance cards

The 18% grey card can be used to ensure perfect exposures when shooting in tricky lighting conditions. Both reference cards can also be used to set a custom White Balance, but how you take a reading off the cards depends on your camera (refer to your DSLR's manual). In the meantime, here is a brief explanation to get you started

DIGITAL SLRS USE sophisticated exposure systems with a choice of metering patterns to suit different lighting situations. The systems work on the assumption that the area of the scene being metered is a mid-tone, or 18% grey to be precise; the average if all dark, light and mid-tones were mixed together. It's the basis of all metering patterns and works surprisingly well, but can render incorrect exposures when the overall scene or subject is considerably lighter or darker than 18% grey. For example, very dark areas or subjects can fool the metering system into overexposing the image, while a very light areas can fool the camera into underexposure, as the light meter will take a reading that renders it as a mid-tone.

As a camera is trying to render an image 'grey', it's your job to ensure you compensate to keep the tones true to life. You can do this by either using one of your camera's exposure override facilities, such as exposure compensation, the AE-Lock button or by metering from an area of the scene that has a mid-tone. And that's where our grey card comes in. Using it is very simple as our step-by-step guide below illustrates.

The key thing to remember is that you need to place the grey card in similar lighting to your subject, for instance, don't place it in a shaded area if your subject is bathed in sunlight. Also, make sure that the card fills the metering area – we would recommend you use spot or partial metering as the card won't need to fill the entire image area – but any is suitable. You can either lock the exposure using your camera's AE-Lock facility or note the aperture and shutter speed, then switch to manual mode and dial in these settings. This latter method isn't suitable on days where lighting is variable. The card has AF reference lines to help your camera's autofocus lock on to it. However, you don't necessarily need it to be in focus to work correctly. The grey card (as well as the white card) can also be used to take a custom White Balance reading from too.

1 GETTING STARTED If you're shooting portraits in difficult lighting conditions, such as backlighting, give your subject the grey card and ask them to hold it angled towards you.

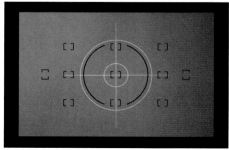

2 TAKE A METER READING Ensure that the entire metering area is filled by the grey card (in this instance we're using spot metering) and lock the exposure with the AE-Lock button.

3 COMPOSE & SHOOT With this exposure locked, you can compose your scene and take your shots. When you check it on your LCD monitor, the exposure should be perfect.